A Retreat with Thomas Merton

By the same author:

CALLED
New Thinking on Christian Vocation

DAILY WE TOUCH HIM
Practical Religious Experiences

CENTERING PRAYER
Renewing An Ancient Christian Prayer Form

CENTERED LIVING
The Way of Centering Prayer

A PLACE APART
Monastic Prayer and Practice for Everyone

MONASTIC JOURNEY TO INDIA

THE EUCHARIST YESTERDAY AND TODAY

IN PETER'S FOOTSTEPS
Learning To Be A Disciple

JUBILEE
A Monk's Journal

O HOLY MOUNTAIN
Journal of a Retreat on Mount Athos

IN SEARCH OF TRUE WISDOM
Visits to Eastern Spiritual Fathers and Mothers

CHALLENGES IN PRAYER

MONASTERY

LAST OF THE FATHERS

POCKET BOOK OF PRAYERS

BREAKING BREAD
The Table Talk of Jesus

A Retreat
with
Thomas Merton

M. Basil Pennington

AMITY HOUSE
WARWICK, NEW YORK

Published by Amity House Inc.
16 High Street
Warwick, NY 10990

Library of Congress Catalog Card Number 87-72466

ISBN 0-916349-23-3

CONTENTS

ILLUSTRATIONS

*Compliments Thomas Merton Study Center; used with permission.

A Retreat with Thomas Merton

FOREWORD

From time to time God in his provident love raises up in our midst a man or woman whose way of being gives to our lives a new hope, a more expansive vision. Thomas Merton, Father Louis of Gethsemani, was such a man. He has spoken and he continues to speak to the hearts of many men and women from very different outlooks and backgrounds. More than anyone else I have ever known, Merton was "Everyman"; he was extraordinarily aware that his life was in some way not just his own, even as he lived with exceptional courage the unique truth of his own inner being.

My personal contacts with Tom were limited. As monks we did not have many opportunities to travel and meet. In the early days even correspondence was strictly limited. Later that was not the case. However, Father Flavian, who was under Merton's guidance as a young monk and later served him as confessor and abbot, believes we can actually get to know Tom better through his writings than we could have through personal contact. Certainly Tom has left us a rich literary heritage. Of all his writings, perhaps his spontaneous, wide-ranging letters,

reveal him most clearly. While I have never ceased to find more and more in Tom's writings, published and unpublished, I have found the tapes of his talks to his novices and his community have given me the best sense of the man: the wonderful humor, the deep humanity, the lively sense of the divine in all and through all. Nothing was foreign to this man who was centered at the Center of the universe. The tapes, even more than the writings, make me aware of the fact that Tom is still very much alive in the Lord and continues to speak to us in a living way.

I undertook the retreat in Tom's hermitage journaled here for a couple very special reasons. I had been to the hermitage many times before and had had some fairly long periods of retreat there. It is a familiar and loved place for me. During this retreat I let that little building with its great hearth and crackling fire, with its expansive porch welcoming all the "neighbors," with its wondrous views across the valley to the abbey and across the knobs to the distant hills, speak to me in its own way. Through it, Tom, who molded it and enspirited it, was present to me in a very special way. Through his books and monographs I heard again his words; through his tapes I heard his voice; in the chapel, before the fire, on the porch, I communed with his spirit.

I had come to the hermitage at the end of a couple years of rather intensive living with Merton in his writings. I was preparing to write a book about him. It was to be biographical, but not in the narrational or historical sense. A number of biographies of that sort had been written, and the "authorized" one was just about to make its appearance. My book would be a "monastic" biography, the story of a journey of the spirit. I had come to the hermitage to sit with Tom for a bit and discern the focus for his story. During those days on Mount Olivet (the name the Gethsemani monks of old had given the particular hill on which the hermitage stands), the focus for our book — ours, for Tom was really writing it with me — became very clear.

I had also come to the retreat seeking clarity in another matter. It was one in which Tom, more than anyone else, could help me. Like him, I found myself a Cistercian monk and a writer. I, indeed, thought I had left my writing behind when I entered the monastery in 1951. And for some years I had, apart from minor translation projects for my brothers. Like Tom's novice master, mine did not encourage any literary activity and there was hardly time for any in those early years of building an abbey and studying for the priesthood. It would be fifteen years before unexpected circumstances would find me publishing again. In the succeeding twenty years, writing — and its concomitants: contacts, correspondence, invitations, lectures — came to occupy more and more of my time and attention. Now I wanted to see if I could resolve some of the ambiguities of this dual vocation. To what extent, under the guidance of Father Louis, I succeeded, it yet remains to be seen. But the retreat did have its moments of light.

I decided to share this little journal for a number of reasons. I have already published several journals. The response to the first one was a revelation to me. *O Holy Mountain* was the journal of my six months on Mount Athos, the holy mountain and monastic enclave at the heart of Orthodoxy. That book actually contained three elements: personal struggles and reflections, some ecumenical theology and dialogue, and a travelogue of a most fascinating place. To my surprise, almost all the reader response was to the first element, the personal sharing. The response to the succeeding journals, *Jubilee* and *Monastic Journey to India*, confirmed that fellows travelers felt that they benefited from my sharing. It is always good to know that we are not alone in the struggles of life. We can support one another in the faith by our honest witness.

Besides sharing my own personal struggle and quest, the pages of this journal also share a good bit of Father Louis's journey. Listening to his tapes and reflecting on some of the monographs stacked on the bookshelves in the corner of the hermitage, I had valuable new insights into his mind and heart. These insights ask to be shared.

Finally, there is a certain amount of quotidian and intimate lore that colors the picture of Merton and his surroundings

— lore that I think will interest his many readers. The Abbey of Gethsemani moves on as it, like the rest of the Church, works at renewal with both aging monks and new ones. Some things have changed; many remain the same. On the paths through the woods, sitting before the fire, watching my feathered friends on the porch, and offering Mass on the cedar altar whose construction Tom had so carefully overseen, I deeply sensed Tom's presence. The details of the hermitage and its environs spoke of his passing, but he had gently left messages in the things that he valued.

I hope what I share in these pages will be a joy and a blessing for you. I want to express my heartfelt gratitude to the abbot and monks of Gethsemani for their many kindnesses and their superb hospitality. They are true brothers. I also want to thank my own brothers, who have supported my literary endeavors and have so generously indulged my needs by allowing me to go to Gethsemani. Above all, I want to thank God for the wonderful gift of Father Louis, Thomas Merton. He has, indeed, been a benediction to me. May his prophetic mission continue and ever expand, fostering ever deeper and richer life among God's people.

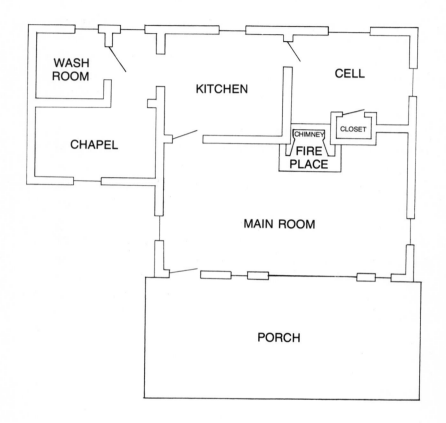

Merton's Hermitage

Sunday, December First

A good day to start a retreat, the first Sunday of Advent, New Year's Day in the Church's liturgical calendar, a time for new beginnings.

I offered Mass this morning with the community of Gethsemani in their century-old basilica — so different from the church at Spencer. It fairly soars with its stark I-beams reaching unimpeded to the austere Romanesque roof. Lightsome even on a gray winter's day. Whitened brick and numerous lances. It must have been quite a change for Tom from the mellow warmth of the previous era of pseudo-Gothic stone. In *The Spirit of Simplicity* Tom lauded the simple, austere beauty of the surviving twelfth-century Cistercian churches. He loved the authentic medium unadorned. The uncovering of Gethsemani's native brick walls must have brought a disappointment to him and others. The brick was found to be too fragile to stand on its own and had to be covered with a protective white coat. All is now open and exposed. Gone are the little chapels around the apse where a monk could slip into a dark corner and pray in secret.

> The Church . . .
> Is half destroyed
> Laid bare by
> Too much light and air
> As though by a cyclone.
>
> Gethsemani, May 19, 1966

I don't know if the monks could live with it if they did not have their private rooms where they can pray to the Father in secret. When darkness descends upon the church and the only light is the flickering lamp between the cross and the tabernacle, then the lofty basilica invites one to enter and offer the silent, secret prayer of the heart.

After none, Brother Anthony, my guide and solicitous

brother, and I descended the escarpment — down the steep stone steps to the valley, across the creek near the glass-fronted water purification plant, and then up the winding dirt road through the woods and along the fields. Across the knobby terrain at some distance we could see the stand of evergreen that turns the field in front of Father Flavian's hermitage into a Zen-like garden. This disciple of Father Louis, who became his abbot, can see from his cell the stand of pine that surrounds his teacher's little cement block house.

The hermitage is not impressive nor particularly beautiful. An open porch — the playground of hungry squirrels and birds — runs the length of the building, some twenty-six feet. Its shed roof shelters the entrance and the picture window in front of the work table. The view is generally in the direction of the abbey to the south, but the woods hide the buildings and the vista reveals only the fields, woodlands, and knobs that lie east of the monastery. The other sides of the hermitage are enclosed by the surrounding woods. It seems a quiet spot that could be many, many miles from anywhere. The tall tree-trunk cross that commands the clearing in front of the hermitage is the only man-made sign that this is a holy place. The little plaque, *Shalom*, hanging by the door, is redundant. Everything whispers "Peace."

****

What do I want to get out of these days of retreat?

> Some renewing experience of God and contemplative time.
> Some clarity on my vocational question.

Already it seems to be coming clear. Maybe that is just proof that I need more prayer and listening. My spiritual father doesn't see it as being so simple. He sees the great need of contemplatives to respond to the growing contemplative aspirations of the laity — not to speak of priests and active religious — even, if need be, at the cost of giving up their own communities and perhaps creating new communities. I may be too ready to let all such ideas and ministry go in order to be free to settle quietly in community. That is, until I get a request like the one from the bishop of Santa Lucia, detailing the great needs of his priests and people. Then my heart longs to reach out and respond. I need to pray a lot more on this; I need to think, write, and talk with friends and advisors.

What else do I want from these days of retreat?

A deeper entrance into the spirit of Thomas Merton. A significant start on the book.

The book — a personal quest, with Tom as guide, into the meaning of true freedom for myself as a Christian and monk; for the Order — or more correctly for the communities in the Order, for each community has its own responsibility; and for the Church, which seems to be in a critical moment with a forceful leader giving a particular interpretation to the spirit of Vatican II, a particular application affecting the Christian life of over 850 million persons. How does a responsible Christian answer to this leadership freely, without undue subservience (motivated by a quest for false security or by the need for recognition within the institutional structures) and without reaction, which is as enslaving as succumbing to domination?

In reflecting on Tom's life and on his quest for true Christian freedom, ever more deeply understood, what answer or direction do I perceive for my own quest? And what can our own communities learn from Tom now? What does he have to say to the Church today?

****

I need to make a couple of decisions: What kind of schedule do I want to follow during this retreat? How much fasting do I want to do?

To a great extent Tom observed the schedule of the community when he lived here in the hermitage. Father John Eudes told me of finding Tom's schedule, written out on a small sheet of paper. It had been left in the breviary he was using in his last months in the hermitage. It had been written up during that last summer of Tom's life, when he was working on *The Climate of Monastic Prayer*. We had started Cistercian Publications in May of that year, 1968. The abbots wanted Tom to be the general editor, but he declined. I took on the job and Tom agreed to be on the editorial board. We decided our first book in the Cistercian Studies Series would be an amplified version of the article Tom had written five years earlier, which had been published in *Cistercian Studies*. In the rewriting it became a general treatment on prayer. The later chapters, with their insightful treatment of dread in prayer, were autobiographical, an expression of the experience Tom went through in the early sixties. Tom did not like to write in the first person about his prayer experience, so the matter is presented in a more impersonal or abstract way, but it flows from deep personal experience and has all the urgency that that kind of experience brings. Tom got the manuscript to me just before he left for Alaska and Asia. The last note I got from him, a postcard from Singapore, was about the galleys for it. The card arrived a few hours before the call announcing his death.

But to get back to the schedule. I think I will basically follow his schedule. A Cistercian, even in a hermitage, is a community man, attached to an abbey. I will move with the prayer rhythm of the community across the valley, beginning with vigils at 3:15 a.m. But I might put off compline till later than 7:40 p.m. because I don't need seven hours of sleep. Since this is a time of retreat for me, after lauds and Mass at 5:45 a.m., I will spend much of what would be work time listening to Tom on tapes and in his books. Brother Anthony brought up a large collection of tapes of the talks Tom gave the novices and the community during the last years of his life. I decided before I came that I would read again Tom's *Thoughts in Solitude.* But first I want to listen to the talk he gave the community on August 20, 1965, the day he left the novitiate to move full time into the hermitage.

I think I have written enough for now. It is time to *be.*

****

I am sitting on the porch. A whipping storm has just passed; the clouds are still low and running, with sun from the west breaking through the layers. The evergreens are catching the harmony of the wind. There is a freshness in the air but yet a tingling chill. Just enough to make a coat comfortable. The blue is winning out as the clouds continue running to the east. The view from the porch! — I wonder how Tom ever wrote anything, or anything but poetry. Each season, each day, must have its own unique beauty. Right now it is the changing sky that commands all. The distant knobs are lost in deep shadow. Bird calls, unfamiliar to my ear, come through when the trees are quiet. This is indeed a place which the Lord has made. May he be praised and glorified in it!

Down at the Abbey, the Blessed Sacrament is exposed on the altar. It is the first Sunday of the month, retreat Sunday. Back home it is a day of great silence, a good way to begin a year.

****

I can see now why Tom was in search of a more remote place. I didn't realize that the hermitage is so exposed. There is only a thin line of trees behind it, then an open field out to the highway. A man appeared from around the side of the hermitage. He said he saw the roof from the road and came up across the fields to see Merton's hermitage. I gently suggested I was on retreat but he persisted and finally asked to make a general confession. I wonder how often during this week I will have "visitors." Anthony said it might snow. That will help. But today is a beautiful day for being out. It has almost the feel of one of those early March days when the winds give promise of warmer days ahead. How capricious nature can be, but captivatingly so.

I think I will go in and start a fire before the house gets too cold. The sun has fallen behind the rise. It soon will be dark.

****

I feasted on Trappist cheese, the special smoked cheese that I like so much, and homemade whole wheat bread. And I listened to a tape of the talk Tom gave the day he left the novitiate to take up full-time life here on the hill they call Mount Olivet. He noted that he spent his whole monastic life in formation: two years as a novice, ten years as novice master, nine as a student, and three years as student master. Now he was graduating to a hermitage.

In the talk, Tom tells of an experience he had during his Easter retreat here at Gethsemani in 1941. He stood just about where the road now leads up to the hermitage and, looking in the direction of the Abbey with its enclosing walls, said to himself, "This place is absolutely out of the question. How can I live in a place like this? You never get out into the woods." Like most of us, most of the time, he was looking in the wrong direction. Already he was sensing the direction in which he was called and had to go. Already his deepest self longed for the freedom of the woods. His desire for this would surface more and more and would take on many false interpretations before he would find his way. "Seek and you shall find." Tom makes it clear in his talk (as Dom James insisted when he spoke with me) that he did not force the abbot on this matter. Nor was it a reluctant grant on the abbot's part. It is true that when Tom spoke of the hermitage back in 1955, Dom James did get permission to allow him to experiment with an eremitical life, but he was not keen about it and was happy when Tom volunteered for the job of novice master. Tom never regretted that choice. Dom James asked him for a three-year commitment to the job. Tom in fact stayed with the novices for ten years. In his departing talk he declared that novice master was the best job in the monastery.

By 1965 he was ready to leave it and go into a hermitage. And Dom James, who himself was moving unobtrusively towards retirement into a hermitage, was ready for Tom to go ahead. He had quietly prepared the way, first allowing a little construction shed to be moved so that Tom could find some solitary hours in it. Then he allowed this cinder block house to be built on the hill. Gradually he allowed Tom to spend more and more time here, eventually to sleep here and come down to the monastery only for his duties as novice master.

Father Louis asserted that the community needed a hermit and that he was delighted that he was the one chosen. As he saw it, it is necessary that the monks realize that there is leeway for the individual vocation within the monastic life. The community, each monk, needs to be reminded and to know that he has his own personal call and the freedom and the responsibility to follow it. Tom's word was that it is necessary that the monk "feel" he has some leeway: an inner sense, something deeper than just knowing, a living sign in the life of a brother that you can follow the movement of the Spirit in the way you live your own life — that you are free.

This points to something specifically Cistercian in Tom's eremitical vocation. Every true hermit sees his call within the context of the Church, for the Church, a witness to the Church. The Cistercian, as one bonded to a particular community by a solemn vow of stability, sees his vocation as within his community even as he draws apart physically from it. He is of his community and for his community, as a sign, a source, and a center.

Tom saw another valuable witness that the eremitical life gives us: "Some assurance that it is possible to put away all care, to live without care, to not have to care." He went on to explain that the care he was speaking of here is useless care, self-defeating care. He was speaking of a life that cannot face death and fills itself with a multitude of things to avoid facing death. The hermit puts aside all care, because he is embracing death, i.e., death to the world. Thus he finds the freedom to live without fear of death.

All of this is, of course, in support of finding that freedom to which all monastic life and all Christian life is dedicated: self-abandonment, a continual forgetfulness of self that leaves the soul free to love God, completely untroubled by the fears, regrets, and anxieties that self-absorption brings. At the same

time, Tom would be the first to admit that we fall far from this ideal and are all too prone to fill our lives with petty cares. But God offers to take on all our cares. Through his Apostle Peter he tells us: "Cast your cares upon the Lord, for he has care of you." Love cares for the other. We care for God and he cares for us.

****

As much as a community needs a hermit, I think it also needs some who are reaching out to the world. Tom, in his extraordinary, paradoxical way, did both. The community needs an incarnational reminder that our lives are not just for ourselves but for the Church and the world, that our lives are meant to bear fruit for the Church and the world. The first Cistercian Fathers, especially those canonized as our models — Bernard of Clairvaux, Aelred of Rievaulx, and Peter of Tarentese, were great examples of this. There can be no doubt about the impact of Cistercian life on the twelfth-century Church and world through these great monks. Enclosed monks are in constant danger of becoming enclosed upon themselves. We need the challenge of a brother who is reaching out in compassion to others and, yes, even letting the pains of the world in to tear at and disturb his contemplative heart.

****

After compline I stepped out into the night. A cloud covering must have come over, for no stars were visible. A few lights shown from the distant knobs. A monastery light could be seen through the woods. The trees still murmured with the rhythms of the winds. But all else was silent. I am ready for bed. I will end this first day of retreat by making Tom's prayer to God our Father my own:

Whatever may have been my particular stupidity, the prayers of your friends and my own prayers have somehow been answered, and I am here. For it is here, I think, that you want to see me and I am seen by you. My being here is a response you have asked of me, to something I have not clearly heard. But I have responded, and I am content: there is little more to know about it at present. Here you ask of me nothing else than to be content that I am your child and your friend. Which means simply to accept your friendship because it is your friendship and your Fatherhood because I am your son. This friendship is Sonship, and is Spirit. You have called me here to be repeatedly born in the Spirit as your son. Repeatedly born in light, in knowledge, in unknowing, in faith, in awareness, in gratitude, in poverty, in presence, and in praise. To be here with the silence of Sonship in my heart is to be a center in which all things converge upon you. This is surely enough for the time being. Therefore, Father, I beg you to keep me in this silence so that I may learn from it the word of your peace, and the word of your mercy and the word of your gentleness to the world: and that through me perhaps your word of peace may make itself heard where it has not been possible for anyone to hear it for a long time.

****

Monday, December Second

When I woke up there were enough coals still alive in the grate to enkindle the fire. I never cease to wonder at fire — how it releases the stored energy and warmth of decades of sunshine. It is blowing colder this morning. The hermitage is in no way insulated, just a cinder block wall. There is a wood-burning stove in the corner, put in years after Tom's passing. But for the moment I am depending wholly on the fireplace as did Tom — quite a task for a fireplace, for the main room is about twenty-four feet long and about fourteen feet wide and has lots of windows.

****

For a second reading at vigils I listened to one of Tom's tapes. His talks are always full of humor — even those on very serious topics like the one I listened to this morning on moral freedom. He was using Abelard as his foil. As usual, he comes out on the side of the underdog. He shows the contribution that that errant monk was making, even while he corrects Abelard's exaggerations. Tom opens his talk by saying that freedom is the most characteristic modern problem, a very important one, central to the problem of meaning. The power of self-determination is basic to the person. When the person takes responsibility for deciding, and for the consequences of his decision, he is mature. Tom sees in Abelard a weakness prevalent today: too much emphasis on intention, making it almost the exclusive determinant of guilt or merit. If one acts with a good intention, we think the action is justified, no matter what it is. In Abelard's day this balancing emphasis on intention was needed because the tendency then was to place all the weight on the side of "objectivity." Today we need to work at keeping a certain objectivity in our moral decisions. We need to avoid being wholly subjective, especially in a time when we are increasingly aware that our actions are often prompted by many unconscious motivations. True freedom lies in the appropriate relationship to reality; i.e., a clear perception of what reality is, and the ability to make responsible judgments and decisions in the light of that perception.

****

Already I can hear the great bells from the Abbey announcing lauds and Mass. The quiet time goes by quickly here, sitting before the fire with coffee, very conscious of God's presence. I really haven't made space yet for wholly free, deep prayer; there is still too much thinking. I will have to do that after Mass. On second thought, I think I will just put off lauds and take some time now.

****

What about fasting? Tom, at least in his last years, was not into fasting. He once joked when weighing in for a Red Cross blood donation that his "icon" was getting a bit out of shape. The pictures of him from the Gethsemani centenary celebration in 1948 and at his ordination in 1949 show a lean enough monk, almost emaciated. The rigorous fasts that were required before Vatican II and the strain that accompanied them pretty much ruined his digestive system, just as they affected the health of many other monks. In Tom's later years he welcomed "care packages" from friends like Naomi Burton Stone. He appreciated it when visitors arrived with six-packs and hamburgers. In this he was not unlike other Cistercians I know.

Tom didn't write much on fasting, but in some notes he wrote in mid-1968 to complement an exchange of letters with Coleman McCarthy in *The National Catholic Reporter*, he did write about the role of discipline in our lives. Discipline can and usually should, if we have the health, include fasting.

In these notes on discipline Tom speaks of fasting only once and then in passing. He emphasizes more the other disciplines of the monastic life: community life, solitude, ascesis (which can include fasting), work, *lectio*, quiet prayer, liturgy, and meditation. But all that he says, I think, can fully apply to fasting.

Tom doesn't deny some of the more popular explanations justifying ascetical works, but he doesn't put much weight on them. Fasting is a good work and has its reward. Jesus fasted, setting the example — imitating him in the proper way is always good — and he said that we, his disciples, would fast. A *quid pro quo* rationale — I'll do this for God and he will reward me — doesn't appeal much to Tom. Or to any of us. It isn't the kind of relationship we have or want to have with our God. Tom speaks of it as a "materialistic view."

For Tom there was a need to respond to tradition. Christians, especially monks, have always fasted. In itself this is enough of an argument to support fasting. We need to enter into the practices of the living tradition and make them our own until they reveal their inner meaning to us. Only then will we be able to be part of the living tradition ourselves and make our contribution, creating the fitting expression of these values for our own times so that we can pass them on as a living reality to those who are following us in the tradition. If we refuse to make these practices our own until we understand them, we may never succeed in understanding them. The meaning of some things can only be discovered from within. With our refusal, traditions can die. They will not survive to be handed on. We have a responsibility to be, first, courageous and self-sacrificing learners and, then, courageous re-creators. To be the latter often takes more courage. Once we have learned the inner value of a practice, we are fearful of losing it by giving it new form. Yet, if it is to stay alive as a tradition, it must be reformed from generation to generation; otherwise we will soon have a lifeless mummy.

We monks have a commitment to fasting in our vow to live the monastic way of life. Every disciple of Christ has a commitment to follow him in his fasting. Ours calls for a clearer expression, to give our sisters and brothers witness, to support them in their fidelity.

One of the reasons that tradition has seen fasting as important is that it fosters our growth in moral virtue and strength. Restraining a very basic appetite, mastering it for the sake of reason, makes us more human; restraining it for the sake of Christ makes us more faithful and loving. We hear our Master's words: "Not by bread alone does one live," and we seek to experience this deep within ourselves. We sublimate a gnawing hunger (I must admit I am not to that stage yet!) to a hunger for the Bread of the Word, the Bread of Divine Life.

Another facet that speaks to me today, though it is not mentioned by Tom in his notes, is a sense of solidarity with the hungry, my sisters and brothers in many lands, young and old, very young and dying before they know what life is. Since I visited Haiti two years ago, the hungry live with me: the most wretched slums I have ever seen — worse than anything I have seen in India or the Philippines — and so near to our own shores. And so much our fault. For years our marines occupied the beautiful island, destroying its native economy instead of building it up. I am grateful for Food for the Poor and what little it can do to alleviate some of the killing and crippling hunger in Boston and Brooklyn and Tokyo, and the slums around Port-au-Prince. (Such an ironic name the manufacturers of these slums have given to their handiwork!) I am, too, with those in the slave camps of Siberia and the hunger camps of Somalia — with my hungry sisters and brothers everywhere.

The value of discipline — fasting and all the other disciplines — which Tom highlighted in his notes is in their role of enabling us to die to our own selves, to transcend the routine person trapped in self-seeking and conventional social living, so that we can rise to the Christ-life animated by the Holy Spirit and be one with Christ. Fasting, discipline, can free us from our passions, our appetites, our emotions, our pseudo-needs, and even from the gripping of real needs which limit, hamper, and ultimately frustrate us. Fasting and discipline open the space for us to be more honest with ourselves, perhaps even to come

to full honesty, so that we can respect ourselves. Fasting cultivates certain inner conditions of awareness and openness that enable us to be ready for the new and unexpected. When we are free from self and the need for security, we can welcome new possibilities and enter into them. The lack of any real discipline in our lives has been perhaps the greatest reason that we have not truly, freely, and generously entered into the great renewal to which the Holy Spirit has been summoning us so insistently since his outpouring in the days of Pope John XXIII and the Second Vatican Council.

There are certainly ample reasons for us Christians to fast and to persevere in fasting. The Woman of Peace who has been appearing at Medjugorje has laid great emphasis on this spiritual practice, asking even the teenagers to fast two days a week on bread and water — which they are doing! Can we monks do less?

Given all this, I think I will settle for tea or coffee, at least for the first couple of days, and see if it will leave me freer to hear the Lord. In any case, it will deliver me from trying to prepare some sort of meal in the rather primitive kitchen here.

****

"Look after me, God, I take shelter in you."
— Psalm 16:1

"For me, the reward is to see you face
and on awakening to have my fill of your likeness."
— Psalm 16:11

****

The temperature has fallen to twenty and we are getting some snow flurries. I brought in a supply of wood and put out some bread (since I am not going to be eating much) and seed for the birds. I put a kettle on top of the wood stove to keep hot water available.

At Mass I found myself often reverting to the Latin text. I guess I am like Tom in that. A dozen years of using that text daily created the space within it to be freely for God. I can appreciate the difficulty old priests have in letting go of it. But if we are offering Mass for the people, our ministry is for them. We have been ordained to a ministerial priesthood. We have to let go of our own preferences and our own spiritual benefits when we are ministering. Peter wanted to stay on Tabor but Jesus led him back down to the plane and told him to hold the secrets of Tabor in reserve for another day and hour. The priest needs his Tabor each day if he is to minister well. He needs to go into his own room and close the door and pray to his Father in secret. When he is free from ministerial responsibilities, he can offer a solitary Mass for and with the whole human family, holding that family in as intimate a style as he wants. But when he is in the midst of his people, he needs to think of those whom he is leading to the Father.

****

The small chapel, twelve feet by seven, the washroom and the little corridor between them were added on to the hermitage later. Little of the heat from the main room reaches them. The bathroom has a small electric heater to keep the pipes — and the monk user — from freezing. The chapel is not so blessed. There is a small Navajo rug on the floor, the one Tom brought back from his visit to New Mexico in May of 1968. The altar is made of cedar. Tom very carefully oversaw its making. And there is a cedar credence in the corner. On the wall behind the altar is a display of icons. Central, as one would expect in a Cisterican chapel, is one of the Holy Mother of God holding her child. It seems to be a rather ancient icon, suffering the ravages of time. Curiously, it is painted on two pieces

of wood joined together which, with the drying of the years, have produced a crease a little off center. This icon is flanked by two icons of the prophet Elijah. Evidently he was the patron of this chapel as he is of the Byzantine chapel at Spencer. These are reproductions of the classical icons of Elijah in the cave and flying off to heaven in his fiery chariot while Eliseos grabs his cloak. Over the credence there is a copy of the Rublev icon of the Trinity. On the other side, above the tabernacle, there is an old triptych. This icon is pictured in Bob Daggy's edition of *Day of a Stranger.* The Mother of God with her child holds the central panel. On the left wing is Saint George, mounted, plunging his spear into the dragon, above whom is Saint Nicholas in his classical pose. On the opposite wing is Saint George's Eastern counterpart, Saint Dimitrius, also mounted and dispatching the foe. Above him is a long-bearded monk, Saint Charalambos. The tabernacle is a small, painted, metal box, fixed to the wall. On the front of it there is an unusual sunburst; eyes and nose and mouth adorn the sun. With all its simplicity, there is a profound sense of prayerfulness in this little chapel. It was a great joy to offer Mass here. I had a sense of a great company with me, all those saints in the icons and many more, and all those dear to me, the communities of Gethsemani and Spencer, and the whole human family. A hermit's Mass is always at the heart of the Church and of creation. I know a hermit who has a globe on his altar when he offers Mass, keeping the most troubled spots on the earth before him as he offers the redeeming Sacrifice.

****

I took time this afternoon to pray the fifteen decades of the rosary. It is a good prayer. It certainly brought my mother to self-giving holiness. Tom, in the schedules he wrote for himself while living here in the hermitage, always made time for the rosary. I haven't used it much in recent years — just sort of used it to fill empty spaces, not taking time for it. The beads are always in my pocket and on my bed. My friend Rose Marie brought me a new rosary from Medjugorje last week. I have been touched by Mary's insistence there — not only the persistence of her visits every night for well over four years, but of her very traditional teaching. I think of those teenagers, especially Ivan, with all the usual struggles of adolescence and then the added challenge of a daily visit with the Mother of God and all the unceasing attention of the pilgrims. I am sure Mary is taking care of her children — but it is in her own curious way. She is so like her Son. Vicka now has a brain tumor. And Ivan flunked out of the seminary — he couldn't manage the Latin. You would think Mary would have done better by him than that!

Mother, you are a hard woman to figure out (but then I guess every woman is — aren't we all? Images, expressions of the infinite God) but I love you all the same. I am happy that I am your monk.

****

Reading *Thoughts in Solitude*. In the preface written in 1956, Tom stresses the importance in our times for independent voices to be heard. He lists Christian saints, Oriental sages (such as Lao Tse), Zen masters, and men like Thoreau, Martin Buber, and Max Picard (who greatly influenced Tom's *Thoughts*). All of these, with the possible exception of Buber, still stand on the bookshelves in this room.

It is interesting, the books that are on the shelves here. Of course, there is no way of telling how many of them go back to Tom's time. John of the Cross — Piers's three volumes, well underlined with marginal notes by Tom — certainly is his. The Celtic stuff probably, for this was something he was working on in his last year here. I was delighted to find a booklet of the writings of one of my forebears, Isaac Pennington, a great Quaker spiritual. Quakerism sort of came to Tom with his mother's milk. He always had a great feeling for the Society of Friends. A wonderful contemporary Quaker spiritual, Douglas Steere, who was an observer at the Second Vatican Council, wrote the introduction to the last book Tom prepared for publication, *The Climate of Monastic Prayer*. Another ecumenical offering, the *Preces Privatae* of Lancelot Andrewes, may indicate the influence of Canon Allchin. Medieval spirituality is well represented: there is the wonderful little *Mirror of Simple Souls* from the thirteenth century — this one does have a note in the back in Tom's hand, the *Book of the*

Poor in Spirit, Hilton's *Scale of Perfection,* the *Ancrene Riwle, The Cloud of Unknowing* (and William Johnston's commentary on it with Tom's introduction), and Colledge's *The Medieval Mystics of England.* There is also a good bit from the Byzantine tradition: *Early Fathers from the Philokalia, Writings from the Philokalia on the Prayer of the Heart,* Fedotov's *Treasury of Russian Spirituality,* and a *Manual of Eastern Orthodox Prayers,* within which there is, on a slip of paper, a copy of the Jesus Prayer in Slavonic (with phonetic interlinear). There are such classics as Baker's *Holy Wisdom,* which Tom very much liked, Butler's *Western Mysticism* (taken from the brothers' novitiate, which had been united to the monks' novitiate when Tom was master), and Causade's *On Prayer,* which Tom quoted in his talk to the community the day he entered into full life here. There is a volume of Thoreau and Max Picard's *The Flight from God.* There is quite a stack of Tom's monographs and most of the books he published before he died, marked with his own curious woodcut, "LOUIS," preceded by "FR" on its side and backwards. And there are some of the basics: four Bibles — Douay, Jerusalem in English and French, and a Hebrew Bible, the Rule of Saint Benedict (Grail Edition), the Regulations of the Order, Webster's Dictionary, and *How To Know Your Trees,* which is marked "Cellarer's office."

****

I took a tramp. There seems to be a jogging trail along the edge of the fields and through the woods. To my surprise, I came upon, besides a shrine of Our Lady, two more hermitages. They go in big for hermitages here evidently. They must have at least six or seven. Besides three full-time hermits, this hermitage is booked most of the time. Brother Anthony tells me he tried to get out one day a week to one called the "Ark." Another brother goes out every Saturday night.

It continues to snow gently. There are fascinating ice

formations around the base of some of the weeds — like large clam shells, very white, but translucent and far more delicate than shells.

A courageous but nervous chickadee took a first pass at the goodies I have spread out on the porch. A tough bluejay soon followed, taking command of the situation. Then a red-bellied woodpecker, a scarlet cardinal and his less brilliant wife, followed by a speckle-breasted pecker and a couple of rabbits. A veritable invasion.

****

In a few masterly sentences in the opening pages of *Thoughts in Solitude*, Tom indicates the whole of the spiritual, or more correctly, the human journey. First, we must detach ourselves from things so that we can truly see them. When we do, we see God in them. Then we can begin the quest for God, leaving things behind, going into the darkness. When we find God, we find all things again in him — the hundredfold. But we have a job letting go of things — especially our own creations: our thoughts and images. We try to get God to fit within them. But any "god" who will fit into our thoughts and images will never satisfy our hearts. He is a false god, an idol that we have created. We have to have the courage to go beyond our thoughts and images where, at first, it is very dark. This is the dark contemplation of which Tom speaks elsewhere. This is the initial experience in Centering Prayer: darkness — until the inner eye of the heart opens and adapts to the too brilliant light that is God. This eye is the penetrating eye of love. When it opens, the heart is filled.

I think I shall stop for a while and enter that darkness which is light.

****

...ber			
...)	Mon.	1848	
	Conv.	1863	
	"	1865	
	Mon.	1886	
	Conv.	1919	
	Sub. Diac.	1921	
	Conv.	1930	
	"	1933	
	"	"	
	"	1942	
	Sac.	1949	
	"	1953	

December

Day		Name		Record	Year
28	B.	ALEXANDER		Conv.	1866
11	N.	THEOTIMUS		Sac.	1874
31	B.	THOMAS		Conv.	1877
30	B.	AUGUSTINE		"	1878
18	B.	JULIUS		"	1883
13	B.	WENDELINE, Prob.†		"	1893
27	B.	ISIDORE		"	"
14	N.	GABRIEL		Mon.	1895
19	B.	PETER		Conv.	"
21	B.	MICHAEL		"	1898
25	B.	NICHOLAS		"	1906
29	B.	BENEDICT		"	1915
12	N.	SEBASTIANUS		Sac.	1924
25	B.	FRANCIS		Conv.	1927
5	B.	THOMAS		"	1932
17	B.	GREGORY		"	1947
27	B.	OWEN		"	1949
21	B.	GERARD		"	1965
5	B.	LEO		Conv. Jub	1968
10	N.	LUDOVICUS		Sac	1968
6	FR.	ROGER			1977
29	B.	PACHOMIUS			1978

I live my life in loyalty to you.

— Psalm 26:3

Do I? Or do I betray you in trying to please others — or myself? Lord, help me to see, to know. I do want to live my life in loyalty to you.

****

Today is the anniversary of the event which Tom described as the great enlightenment: his visit to the shrine of the reclining Buddha in the living rock at Polonnaruwa. Many Christians do not feel comfortable following Tom barefoot through the damp grass on the Gal Vihara. They are more at home accompanying him on his pilgrimage to the tomb of the Apostle Thomas, his pocket full of relics. Incidentally, the relics that were with him on that journey are here now in the hermitage chapel. A brother has mounted them in a frame and they sit on a table beneath the tabernacle. It is an interesting collection. There is his patron, not Thomas the Apostle, but Thomas of Canterbury, Thomas à Becket, the English martyr who once sought refuge in a Cistercian abbey. There is another English saint: Bede the Venerable. There is Thérèse of the Infant Jesus, from the Carmel at Lisieux, probably the best-known contemplative in our century. And five hermits: Peter Damian, the reformer of the Camaldolese Order, and Romuald, their founder, an order which Tom once thought he would join; Bruno, the founder of the Carthusian Order, which also attracted Tom; Nicholas of Flue, the patron of Switzerland; and the most recently canonized hermit, Charbel of Lebanon. (In his notebook in 1966 Tom listed the ten relics he then had here. The changes are interesting. He had the four hermits: Peter Damian, Romuald, Nicholas, and Charbel, and also Bede. He did not have Thomas then, but rather Louis. And there were the two great Carmelites: Teresa of Avila and John of the Cross. In addition there was Saint Paul and Saint Basil's good friend, Saint Gregory Nazianzanus.) Significantly though, now mounted around these relics are the saffron prayer beads that Tom received in India. Somehow for Tom all the Western strivings for holiness he had studied, spoken of, written so well of, and sought to live, were drawn together in his Eastern experience and in particular in his experience of Polonnaruwa.

I, too, have climbed that sweep of bare rock, sloping away on the other side of the Gal Vihara, where "you can go back and see different aspects of the figure." As I walk there today in spirit with Tom, I pray that I may be "jerked clean out of the habitual half-tied vision of things" and find that "inner clearness" where "all problems are resolved and everything is

clear." For Tom, it was a moment of completion: "I know and have seen what I was obscurely looking for. I don't know what else remains, but I have now seen and have pierced through the surface and have got beyond the shadow and the disguise." For this alone Tom's whole journey was worthwhile. And I don't mean just the journey to Asia. I mean his whole lifelong quest for true freedom — for now he had found it. The powerful aesthetic beauty of that little valley, its great peaceful sculptures, tore out the heart of the artist and brought him to the beyond. I don't know if, in fact, it really mattered that the sculptures were of Buddha and his disciple. (I was far more touched by the disciple.) It was a moment when manifest beauty, truth, harmony, and being summoned the well-prepared monk into the presence of the Unmanifest more fully than ever before. In 1965, in a moment of special candor with his community, as he was taking his leave to take up full-time residency at the hermitage, Father Louis revealed something of his own transcendent experience (he rarely did this, albeit publisher of many journals): "I know from what experience I have of it so far... that in fact it is sometimes possible to see that things become transparent. They are no longer opaque and they no longer hide God. This is true... We are living in a world that is absolutely transparent; God is shining through all, all the time. This is not just a fable or a nice story. It is true." We have heard his testimony and it is true. This day at Polonnaruwa, what three years earlier was "sometimes possible" and had become more and more possible, became a living reality: "What else remains?" Nothing! The search for true freedom, freedom in the truth, was over.

Perhaps we need to hear again those words of the Lord to Isaiah: "My thoughts are not your thoughts, nor your ways my ways," says the Lord. "But as high as the heavens are above the earth, so high are my ways above your ways and my thoughts above your thoughts." For we are tempted to ask, "Why Polonnaruwa in the shrine of the Buddha?" "Why by electricity, in a Red Cross Conference Center in Bangkok?" Long ago Tom wrote of the burnt men. He wanted to burn out in

the quest. The quest was complete. He was burnt. In his compassion he wanted those of his own West to be enriched by the riches of the East, he wanted the East and the West to be one in peace, harmony, and mutual enrichment. God always gives us what we want — what we really want, not what we say we want; he looks to the heart, not to the lips. But he gives it usually not in the way we want it. At Polonnaruwa, East entered into the West in the person of Father Louis, a monk who had caught the deepest aspirations of the West and expressed them so well that millions identified with what he wrote. East and West came into peace, harmony, and mutual enrichment in this "Buddha" from the West. What he wanted for all, he received for himself as a sacrament for us all, powerfully, symbolically, inviting us all to the same experience.

The vicar general who sat under the tree reading all about the shrine in a guide book while Tom went ahead and entered into the experience that sees "through every question without trying to discredit anyone or anything — *without refutation* — without establishing some other argument," symbolizes so much of our Church leadership. In spite of the powerful leading of the Spirit in the Second Vatican Council. Tom knew that "for the doctrinaire, the mind that needs well-established positions, such peace, such silence, can be frightening." It takes us beyond the security of our well-reasoned definitions and answers that cover over the true, exciting, and challenging mystery of an intimately present, undefinable God. Petty prejudices — the vicar general didn't like "paganism" — close over many areas of God's revelation, avenues that have led "pagans" into profound and transcendent experiences of the Truth that is revealed.

If our Church is to be, indeed, "catholic," then we all, hierarchy and lowerarchy, have to have the courage to leave our secure perches beneath obscuring *Summas*, that pretend to contain all truth within the confines of their syntheses, doctrines, definitions, and formulas. We have to shake off our dislikes and deeper prejudices that constrict our hearts and make them so unlike the universally loving heart of our Master. We need to have courage like Father Louis to take off the shoes of our own customary ways and walk among our brethren of the other faiths and paths, one with them in a common search for peace, harmony, and spiritual enlightenment. It will do us little good to have the right dogmatic answers (the devils know the truth, too) if we do not have that experience of the truth that calls forth from us a complete "yes," that calls us forth from our everyday earth-bound consciousness into the clarity of a compassionate universal love. So long as we do not *love* — and love involves respect, acceptance, and appreciation — any one single human person, we do not love Christ, we are not Christian — for "whatever you do to the least, you do to me." The challenge is clear and great — what we must do — made clear by the life and death of Thomas Merton.

But let me not deceive myself. In responding to the great vision, let me not miss the less dramatic, but perhaps as demanding one, right at home. I need to walk also with my more conservative and my more liberal sisters and brothers and be one with them. (I hate those labels, liberal and conservative, but I use them here because the very challenge is to let them, for all practical purposes, be dissolved in my love.) To accept my sisters and brothers, I do not need to accept all they hold any more than I need to accept all the tenets of my Buddhist sisters and brothers. I do need to accept these persons and love them and be willing to walk with them when it is the call of love to do so. If I can take off my shoes with my Buddhist brothers, I can take off my chasuble with my liberal brother; if I can chant a sutra with my Buddhist sister, I can chant a *Kyrie* with my conservative sister. I may not have Paul's total self-giving that can be all things to all, but I can strive for it. The Lord Jesus comes in *every* woman and man — there are *no* exceptions — and he is my love, my life, and my Lord.

Tuesday, December Third

I woke up early with a headache. The cold and dampness have gotten into my sinuses. A good fire should dispel that.

****

I will instruct you and teach you the way to go. I will watch over you and be your advisor.

— Psalm 32:8

Lord, thank you for this word. I want your help and guidance in discerning how I am to go. Watch over me always.

****

He sees himself with too flattering an eye. To detect and distrust his guilt.

— Psalm 36:2

Lord, help me to see myself as I truly am. Help me to recognize fully and clearly my sinfulness and truly to repent of it.

****

I have been reading in Tom's *Thoughts in Solitude* about the path to Christian contemplation. As I look back I can see how I have stumbled along something like that. Yet I never seem to have consciously tried to follow a path. I have just tried to live the Gospel as it is found in the Rule of Saint Benedict, and to follow the practices of the monastic life each day, as they were presented to me, and to spend time with Jesus-God in thought and prayer and reading. We have been friends, and I might even say lovers. We live together. My life is in him and he is in my life. It is all kind of simple. It has been good and pretty steady. No big deal. Just quiet joy and thankfulness. I kind of like it that way. Centering is the best, but the whole day and night are pretty good, because he is always around. I get pulled out of the center at times. And that usually leads to grief. But the regular Centering gets me back where I belong and restores peace. Thank you, Lord, for so much more than I deserve.

> I offer you praise, O Father, Lord of heaven and earth, because what you have hidden from the learned and the clever, you have revealed to the merest children.
> — Luke 10:22

****

I prayed Psalm 38 at lauds today and heard deeply its call to conversion and repentance. I was thinking especially of celibacy.

> Lord, all that I long for is known to you.
> My sighing is no secret from you.
> My heart is throbbing, my strength deserting me;
> The light of my eyes itself has left me.

Celibacy is not first of all a thing of the flesh but of the spirit. It is the choice to commit myself to God, Christ, to be the love of my life — all other loves being within that love and empowered by it. Life is love. God is love. It is with love that all is ultimately found. All life is to be a school of love. Our quest is ever to grow in love. In this, celibacy and marriage are the same — just different ways. Either we are going to learn and grow by soloing with the Lord in response to a beautiful invitation or we are going to ask another to be with us all the way and make a commitment to her or him and accept his or her commitment so that the two of us are always together in this work of growing in love.

I chose celibacy and committed myself to the Lord in this way by a solemn vow. The solemn vow means I so give myself to the Lord — just like a man who has given himself to a woman — so that I can no longer give myself to anyone else in that marrying way. I am given.

Celibacy is first of all a giving as person. It doesn't preclude other deep loves, relationships, experiences of such love, even appropriate physical expressions. Fidelity to the Lord in this commitment of love does rule out *allowing* any other person or desire from getting such a hold on me that it gets in my way of being wholly to the Lord and of my placing those persons and desires within my relationship with him. I am human. I fall in love. I have desires. In themselves, all these are OK; in fact, they are good. I cannot have too much love in my life. I cannot love too many people and be loved by them too much. Every love can be fostered by and enjoy appropriate physical expressions. But the celibate heart will not *willingly* allow these experiences or the desire for them to interfere with or detract from the complete "yes"to the Lord and the expressions of that "yes" that are due. This is why I need deep prayer — constantly to find the freedom as well as the empowerment and joy that will enable and support me in living my choice and commitment faithfully. Centering Prayer is especially helpful here because my "yes" and all the realizations of that have become associated with a prayer word. When I experience other loves and desires tugging at me in ways that are not in line with my "yes" to my Beloved, I can use the prayer word to be faithful to him and let these other feelings and desires go. Sometimes it takes a lot. But each time I use my prayer word, it is an attempt at saying a wholehearted (a very good and accurate word here) "yes" to the Lord.

When I am well centered in my love, then I can freely love others and enjoy that love and expressions of it. These all come out of that center and are beautiful expressions of and participations in it. I can be a real lover.

All of this holds for a married man when his life is well centered in his love for his wife in God. And the same is true for a married woman. A truly loving couple can be, powerfully, to others in love. But they must first of all give all the time, attention, priority, and energy necessary to cultivate their love for each other in God. As a celibate, I must do that with God.

A celibate is unfaithful if he allows work, service, ministry, or love of others to cut into the time and energy he *needs* to cultivate his primary love-relationship with God. And, in fact, he is undermining his ability to do any of those things in the loving and effective way they should be done.

Michael Mott's rather full reporting of Tom's relationship with Marge raised questions of many. Who are we, anyone of us, to judge another? That Tom was open enough and free enough in his humanity to fall in love is only to be admired. Would to God all monks and priests had such openness and freedom. If Tom willingly allowed the evolving relationship and the desires that went with it to impinge on his complete "yes" to God, then this would be a failure to live to the full his commitment to celibate love. There are indications that this may have been the case at some moments. I think of some of the poetry Tom wrote for Marge (though we must never forget that poetry tends to exaggerate):

> . . .where your heart
> Slept for me
> For me restored itself to life and to the love
> By which alone I keep alive
> For whose essential and direct messages
> I am waiting now pacing up and down
> In this uneasy lonely place
> Waiting once again to live
> And at war with my own heart
> Because I cannot be there
> To see your eyes. . .
> — *Aubade on a Cloudy Morning*

How can I sleep exhausted
In the midst of knowledge

Your gentle love
Still follows me with patient lessons
Quieter than night

Envelopes me and will not let me go
Though you lie alone
Now miles from where I am
And I have only the faint fragrance
Of your lips and long hair
How can I sleep exhausted
Torn out of my dear school...

— *Six Night Letters, IV*

Yet, Tom may have been willing to risk moments of struggle and possibly lapse in pursuit of what he perceived to be a very important good for his growth as the loving man he should be. If we are at all realistic, we know if we do open ourselves to loving others, there is always the probability that feelings and desires will soon arise. Should we then guard against falling in love? Such guardedness can be overdone and lead to truncation as a human person. Allowing the space for love insofar as our commitments allow and being ready — as ready as we can be — to struggle for a proper integration of the feelings and emotions that may well ensue, calls for a lot of courage and self-confidence in the right sense and confidence in God, the love of our life. I think I would rather fall on the side of risking love and the struggle, than risk being too guarded and miss the beauty and loveableness of my brother and sister made by Love. If Tom deliberately chose to open himself to Marge's love and to loving her, it was a courageous thing.

As the Psalm says, "When our hearts start throbbing, the light of our eyes leaves us." At such times, above all, we need another to help us see.

I pray for the courage to remain always open to love, to be a complete "yes" to my Love and to everyone and everything that comes into my life as an expression of his love. And I pray for the wisdom, counsel, and courage to say that "yes" in the way it needs to be said.

****

There is a bit of the Orient in this very Western little building. On one side of the fireplace there hangs a parasol which Suzuki sent Tom; on the other, a beautiful Madonna from Japan — a wonderful blending of the East and the West.

Tom did not speak much of Mary or write much about her. He had a very simple and human devotion to her as mother. Speaking to the novices, he urged them to be perfectly simple, perfectly human in their devotion; to have the emotions of a child without being sentimental. Tom himself wanted to live in total dependence on Mary. We can never be detached from her. Every movement of grace comes through her. This does not detract from Jesus; this is his will. It shows forth the fullness of the incarnation, how completely God has placed his power in the human milieu. In 1962 Tom preached on the Feast of the Immaculate Conception. The priests of the community are assigned different feasts on which to preach to the community. In those days it was only on feasts; now we preach also on Sundays. In his sermon Tom spoke of Mary as light, the woman clothed in the sun, the new Jerusalem. God put man and woman into the material creation as its light, but they were quickly extinguished. In the covenanting with Abraham and then with Moses, God sought to rekindle the light, coming to them in fire. But the people withdrew in fear. Then, in many lesser ways, God sought to make his light present, at least in glimmers, preparing for the time when the Light of the World would come. Mary fully received that light. There was no drawing back, only a complete *fiat* — "Be it as you will." What God wants and will accomplish in all the universe is already accomplished in Mary. This is the meaning of her being drawn up into heaven in her body at the Assumption. She is the Star of the Sea to guide us all home. She is conceived immaculate so that the light can shine through her wholly unimpeded. How beautifully does the Japanese Madonna, with her extraordinary delicateness, bespeak a lamp, a vessel of light, a shrine for the true Light which enlightens us all.

****

There has been shooting in the woods. And from time to time stronger vibrations rattle the windows. I believe these are from the artillery at Fort Knox. I can see more and more why Tom was in search of greater solitude. Now a train cries in the dark. A great owl hoots in the tree west of the hermitage. I hope he doesn't decide to spend the night serenading me.

The sun broke through for a while this afternoon and I took a couple of rolls of film, some slides for the brethren at Spencer, and some black and white my publisher might like to use. It remains quite cold. From the porch I can see across the field a little shrine of the Immaculate Heart of Mary. It is the only man-made thing in sight. I have been doing most of my praying before the fireplace — the chapel has no heat. But as it gets dark, the flickering lamp before the tabernacle beckons to me. Tom told the sisters in Alaska that he did not have the Blessed Sacrament in his first years here and he did not think of it. (The chapel and washroom were added not long before his final departure.) But when he was finally allowed to have the Sacrament, he realized how much he liked to pray in the Presence. He found it consoling when he lay awake at night to realize that the Lord was there with him.

****

The desire is a pledge of the fulfillment of the desire.
— Saint Bernard

****

The sky has cleared a bit; some stars shine fully. The hoot owl has moved to the woods down by the shrine, still within earshot. The air is filled with the cozy odor of wood smoke. Night has come.

Wednesday, December Fourth

The first reading at Vigils today was a text from Isaiah. It is one that must have spoken powerfully to Tom:

> Learn to do good,
> search for justice,
> help the oppressed,
> be just to the orphan,
> plead for the widow.
> Come now, let us talk this over,
> says Yahweh.
>
> Though your sins are like scarlet
> they shall be white as snow;
> though they are red as crimson,
> they shall be white as wool.
>
> — Isaiah 1:17-18

Our white cowls remind us constantly of this cleansing. We long for it. But we do not so readily recall the way to win or rather to open ourselves to this cleansing — the way of mercy and compassion. We need Father Louis, who came to understand this divine dispensation deeply and who lived and wrote of it so well, to remind us. Not even the enclosed monk, who has, indeed, heeded a divine invitation to go apart, can hope to receive the gift of a pure heart if he does not open his heart to compassion, to the suffering and needs of his sisters and brothers. It is only when we open our hearts to others that we are open to receive the cleansing of the divine mercy. "Blessed are the merciful for they shall receive mercy."

****

Epiphany — letting reality be itself to us. Not figuring it out or thinking it through. Just letting it be present, manifesting what it is. What is, is God, revealing his caring love in all. Even when what has been, has been disfigured and desecrated by sinful us, still, if its reality is allowed to shine, then from beneath the disfigurement God appears — is present. To be to this, to let God be to us — this is communion, this is prayer. Nothing more needs to be thought, said, or done. The mutual gift is pure, complete, and unimpeded. This is love: the complete gift of self and openness to the gift of the other. Mutual Epiphany.

****

Day begins in a glimmer — the faintest streak of Easter purple, tending towards pink, along the rim of the eastern sky. The crackling, cheery fire still dominates all. But soon its pathetic little blaze will be lost in a flood of light as the great fire rises to take command of the day. I have turned my back on the comforting hearth as I let the sun's warmth blind my eyes. Day is! What will it bring? Epiphany? Perhaps understanding? Always new hope.

I had a dream. I was walking along a road in India. The man in front of me entered a tower or gateway. As I passed, he emerged and beckoned me in. I was warmly embraced in welcome by his master, a priest I knew well but who in the dream was a faceless friend. Later, as I sat sketching the tower, a walled garden appeared. The tower was a gateway to a garden enclosed.

What does this mean? Whom do I encounter? My deeper self? Or the Lord? The invitation is to go within.

I had another dream. The maid arrived home — a large colonial mansion — to find a motorcycle gang on the porch. She started to chase them away but the mistress of the house emerged and invited them in for breakfast. As they moved about the house, the boys pocketed various things. The mistress told the leader he was responsible for the boys. Then she chided one young lad to put back a silver salt and pepper set. She kissed him and told him that he was a beautiful person.

Someone — is it my abbot or is it my own monitor — is trying to keep the mob, who will take my time and energies, from invading my house. Yet, I welcome them, want to feed them, chide their indiscretions, but affirm their God-given beauty.

Perhaps it is time to look at my question: Do I continue as I have, or do I move away from my activities and seek a more secluded contemplative life? In spite of the fact that my new abbot does not, in general, favor my activities, the year has been one of the most active I have had. I have taught Centering Prayer in monasteries, universities, prisons, and cathedrals, to all sorts of groups from Massachusetts to Florida — mostly east coast this year, though I am scheduled to go to California in June again. I have done radio and television shows, recorded audio and video cassettes, as well as written three books and more articles and book reviews than I can count. On top of all that, the abbot has me raising money for an infirmary for our dear old monks. Along with all that there is the regular life: office in choir, chapters, committee meetings, community meals, events, work in the bookstore, Trappist Preserves, the garden, etc. As I review all this, I am a bit overwhelmed — even exhausted at the thought of it all. But as I lived through it, it didn't seem like so much. I took three or four days each month at the hermitage and time each day for Centering Prayer and *lectio.* In all, my Love (as I write that word, I feel a bit naked — but I don't seem to find any other name for him quite right at the moment) was very much with me. There has been a lot of deep joy and peace, deep flowing waters.

Yet, what is God trying to say to me through my new abbot? The abbot in some very real and significant way holds the place of Christ for his monks. I need to hear what the Lord is saying to me through him.

This is probably a very good place to look at this question

— here with Tom. He went through a long struggle during his early days in the monastery, reconciling himself as a writer with himself as a monk. He wrote a lot about that. That has never been a serious problem for me so far. I am not so grabbed as a writer. I did not return to my writing until I was in the monastery a dozen years. In his last years, especially after Father Flavian became his abbot, Tom was struggling basically with what I am struggling with here — when to say "no." He was harried by hundreds of requests. So long as he had Dom James, he could handle invitations to go out by letting the abbot say "no." But in regard to writing, he was on his own. I pushed him to come on the Board of Editors of Cistercian Publications in May of 1968. He himself volunteered *The Climate of Monastic Prayer* to be our first book. But then I pushed him to write a preface for our second book, Hallier's *The Monastic Theology of Aelred of Rievaulx*. He kept resolving to write no more prefaces, book reviews, and the like. I realize I now have eight book reviews waiting to be done and two manuscripts to be read, besides the page proofs of two of my own books. I have three other books under contract. It is getting to a point that is ridiculous.

I am inclined to draw a line; no more commitments to write anything and no more engagements after August 1. Back to the routine contemplative life. That is my temperament. It is either/or. I am saying "yes" to all that is asked of me or I am closing down completely.

I just realized I wrote "routine contemplative life" — quite a contradiction in terms; if anything, a true contemplative life is never routine; contemplation (a life never should be called "contemplative" if it is not filled with contemplation) is far from routine. It is full of surging life and vitality — all the flow of a divine vitality. It is being fully open and exposed to the divine creative energies. The trouble is that institutional contemplative life — canonical contemplative life — has become for some just routine; it is not filled with contemplation. It is living through the motions of going to choir and standing there distracted, reading books distractedly, keeping busy with work and projects. It is not epiphany. It is this "routine contemplative life" that I abhor. If I need a lot of activity to avoid such a thing, I want to keep active. But I don't think it should be necessary to be continually engaged in conferences and writings, in order to keep my own prayer life alive. I do certainly get some animation and motivation from teaching others. The best way to learn is to teach. I keep getting new insights as I seek to express myself and answer questions. I do a lot of Centering with those I teach (maybe that is getting the silver salt and pepper set back). The Lord has been very good to me, so present and loving in the midst of all this activity. He has never been absent, but always with me in the deeper places.

I had a long talk with Abbot Thomas. He has been tremendously active since he resigned his abbatial charge, teaching a great deal, sharing the Centering Prayer, building spiritual bridges across to the East. He has a strong realization of the decisiveness of our times. The human family needs to find a spiritual unity or it may well destroy itself. The Church is in crisis as many retreat from the challenge of renewal and the evolution necessary to be to a rapidly evolving world. They seek security in centralization and adherence to static formulas that are largely incomprehensible to today's youth or any thinking person. The authority of the local church, the local monastery, has to stand on its own courageously and respond to the reality at hand. If it lets itself be co-opted by central authority, it will cease to be creative of life — the local community will fossilize, which is worse than dying and leaving space for something new.

Let me not attribute these thoughts to Abbot Thomas. These are what I see after talking with him. He sees the urgency of the present — even more now than when Pope Paul VI asked us to do all we could to help the Western Church refind its contemplative dimension. The need for this contemplative dimension is ever greater now. And the openness to it among the laity is far greater. But who is there to teach, to help, to lead? One would immediately think that contemplative communities would be ready to help, but how many of them are really teaching prayer and sharing their contemplation in any effective way? Certainly very few of our Cistercian monasteries. That is why monks like Abbot Thomas and I seem so exceptional. If all monasteries were places where lay persons, priests, and active religious could go to learn the ways of contemplative prayer and to learn how to bring these to others, Thomas and I could easily stay at home in our own monasteries.

There is hardly a real Christian meditation (contemplative prayer) center in the country, while there are many Hindu and Buddhist centers ready to receive any seeker at any time. How soon will it be before we will begin to have Christian meditation centers as an integral part of every diocese, meditation rooms in every parish? Religious who are looking for a more meaningful apostolate for our times should consider this. This could be a very important work that could be done even by retired sisters and brothers. What better use could be made of convents and schools and other buildings that are no longer needed for the works of other active apostolates?

Leadership, of course, should not be restricted to religious. It was young lay persons who brought the charismatic movement into the Catholic Church and back home to the parishes from the campuses. Young adults want to make a contribution; they want to make a difference. Yet in our Church there is little place for the young adult. Parishes are geared to families and children. No wonder some of our most promising young people give their energies to TM, EST, the Moonies, and other movements where their contribution is welcome. Isn't it time we had a powerful Christian Meditation — Centering Prayer — Movement, with our young adults called forth to enthusiastic leadership? It is time for cautious bishops and pastors to take a chance on youth. Or there will be fewer and fewer youth not only in our seminaries but even in our churches. Let young people know that we really want them by summoning them to make their contribution now while they are young and enthusiastic. Then we will have plenty of vocations to the ministries of the Church.

There comes to my mind something that Father Louis wrote a few months before his death:

Anyone who undertakes to be a monk knows that by the very fact of his vocation, he is summoned by God to a difficult, lifelong work, in which there will always be anguish and great risk. If he evades this work under any pretext whatever (even under the pretext of conformity to an exterior ritual or ascetic observance which does not really suit his inner needs) he must know that he cannot have any peace with himself or with God because he is trying to silence the deeper imperative of his own heart.

My abbot certainly wants me to conform to an external ritual and ascetic observance. He wants everyone in the community to do that. He likes the old conformity in a new robe. And a part of me could be very comfortable conforming, especially with the approval of my abbot. But does such observance really suit my inner needs, or do I need to take the risk of pushing ahead in what I am doing even if it doesn't have his wholehearted blessing? I am not talking here of any disobedience. Once the abbot commands, the matter is settled. At least for me. He has to answer to God for his commands. I can rest secure in obeying. (I don't think that is a false security, although some question it.) I can see the possibility that God could call me away from such obedience as he has called others — I think of Mother Teresa of Calcutta leaving Loreto to go to the streets. But I would want to be very sure that it is the Lord calling. But the abbot is not apt to decide everything. He is quite capable of saying "no" and usually does. Yet there is still a lot of space where I must or can decide for myself. That is where the risk lies. Good intentions do not cover everything. Discernment and fidelity are important.

Although my tendency is to be radical and go all the way, one way or the other — to be active, saying "yes" to all that I am asked, or withdraw completely — I suspect the final discernment will be for something in between. That is something that is difficult for me. Perhaps the decision, at least

the long-term decision, is not to be made now. Maybe it would be good to plan on a period of deeper seclusion in the latter part of the coming year during which time I could discern more clearly the course to be chartered in the following year(s).

As I write this, I think of all Tom's searching in his last months, seeking to discern where and how he might find truer solitude. The search was what he was supposed to be about. The finding was in God's hands.

I can see whatever way I choose; it can be a way to greater freedom, greater love. The important thing in the process is to choose freely.

But what if the choice is not left with me? Can I still choose freely and be free? Yes.

Suppose the abbot does decide to make all the decisions. Then I can freely choose to obey him. Christian obedience, evangelical obedience, is embracing, even with a vow, the will of God manifested through the superior for the sake of freedom in the likeness of Christ. With the greatest of freedom, Jesus chose always to do the things that please the Father — that is what I want to choose. He was obedient unto death, even death upon a cross, yet no one took his life from him. He freely laid it down. In obedience, we are freely with God, for he is where his will is.

There is no problem if obedience decides all. But what if in some way I am physically imprisoned? I can hardly imagine myself being thrown into jail — though all things are possible — but I could conceive of myself imprisoned on a sick bed. I have seen that happen to too many people I know and love. What then? Even then I could choose freely, not in the dark way that Sartre would have us choose to be free in the void, accepting the thrownness of the world without any relation to it. Not in the way of Epictatus and the Stoics — in some way accepting providence. But in the full Christian way of accepting what happens as the choice of the Beloved, the place of encounter chosen by him. Things don't just happen. Ultimately, God is in charge. He has everything under control. How ontologically this all works out with full respect for human freedom, I don't pretend to understand. After all, God is a bit — to say the least — beyond me. I accept; no, more, I freely embrace what *is* because of his free choice.

In that choosing I remain free and grow in freedom, living that choice as many, or at least some, have learned in the concentration camps and are now learning in the slave camps of Siberia, in the prisons around the world, on death row, in the starvation camps of Africa and the slums of Port-au-Prince, and in innumerable other "prisons." No one can take our freedom from us. Only we can choose — and it is a free choice — to give it up — at least as long as we have human life. If

we lose our life, we will be eminently free. If we lose our humanity, our rationality, our captors will have, in fact, only our bodies, for our spirit will elude their grasp. Inner freedom, like its divine prototype, is a thing of the spirit.

In freedom, then, I will choose in order to be ever more free.

****

The view out the window over the work table is truly special: the fields sloping down to the hedgerow, the loblolly pines scattered through the valley, the woods behind them on the nearest knobs, and then misty valleys and hills stretching away to the horizon. The sky is soft, hues of blue and gray, with white where the clouds thin out — all very still. The far misty valley draws — to peace, to quiet, to contemplation. A most gentle epiphany.

****

At the end of the last talk he gave in Alaska, Tom said, "If someone is living in an unconditional "yes" to God's love, he or she is fully living what they came to religion for. Nothing else really matters once that is taken care of." The question: Is my "yes" unconditional? I want it to be. It is no use raising up all sorts of scenarios as if I am ready to do this or that. I don't have the grace to do the imaginary — only the real. But the conditions we place are usually unconscious. We have to catch them. Usually someone else is better at spotting them. Here is where a spiritual father or mother or friend can help. We are quick to rationalize, making our conditions into principles and arguing that "I have to be true to myself." That ruse needs to be uncovered, so that I can be a complete unconditional "yes." Lord, help me.

****

One of the things I think the Church can learn from Thomas Merton — I am thinking here of the teaching Church, bishops and priests — is how effectively to do just that: to teach. Our Lord's final command to the apostles was to go forth and teach. It is a primary duty for the apostles' successors and those who join them in their ministerial ordination. Tom was and is an effective communicator of the Good News. I do not think any Catholic author has ever reached a larger audience. His books continue to sell and sell, as do tapes of his talks. Hundreds of other writers are engaged in making his message heard and in translating him into a multitude of languages. Every publisher is happy to have Merton material.

What are the qualities that make Tom such an effective and attractive communicator of the Truth?

More fundamentally, there is his *openness,* an expression of his freedom in the Spirit. He kept open to every channel of truth and he constantly drew on a vast array of sources. He was *up to date* and *well informed.* He knew whereof he spoke. He proclaimed the absolute centrality of the Paschal Mystery, fully in the context of our times. He constantly read and read widely. He listened and he called forth response.

A busy bishop or pastor might say, "All well and good for a man who enjoys the leisure of the contemplative life. But I don't have the time to read."

Tom's life was not so leisurely. He made the time and he made choices. For over ten of his very productive years he held the second most important position in one of the largest abbeys in the world. He was always vitally concerned and vitally involved in all that went on in his community and in his worldwide order. Yet he never allowed himself to become provincial or even merely ecclesial. He did keep up an active participation in all that concerned the universal Church. He wrote to popes and bishops and to the laity at large. He followed closely all the developments of the Council. He kept up with Catholic theology and Orthodox and Protestant theology as well. And he is well known for his outreach to other spiritual traditions. The whole world was his because it was Christ's and because he was a member of the human family — the family of God. He kept up to date on political events, especially all that concerned peace, social justice, and racial equality. He was well informed about Marxism and communism. Nothing human was foreign to him. So that when he proclaimed the Good News, his hearers knew that he was speaking to them, speaking into the context of their lives and not from some detached ecclesiastical realm. Even though he was a monk who had chosen to live apart. He lived apart, but he was at the heart of things.

Although Tom was well read and well informed, his message always remained *personal.* He never sought to impress or overwhelm with his erudition. He never simply passed on learning. He shared what he had assimilated and related, in the fabric of his own being, with the central reality of the cross, death, and resurrection of Jesus as Lord. His message was always existential, in the best meaning of the word. His teaching came out of what he believed enough to live and, in the living, found to be truly life-giving.

Finally, Tom *respected his hearers,* whom he loved. He respected their time, their intellects, their sophistication, and their simplicity. Above all, he respected their freedom. He never came on with threats, he never tried to force anything down anyone's throat. Rather he let the Truth, which he shared out of love, speak for itself and call forth its own assent.

Our Lord told us we are to be perfect even as our heavenly Father is perfect, adding, "He lets his rain fall on the just and the unjust alike." Rain comes down in many ways. It may be a driving storm. But I suspect the Lord was thinking here of that gentle rain spoken of by the prophets. Whatever way it comes, though, the receiver is free to receive it as he will. He can hide from it and ignore it , or he can welcome it and use it for cleansing or to slake his thirst. God respects our freedom. His worthy minister will do the same.

The breadth, the depth, and the manifest love of Thomas Merton have won for him an enduring and eager audience. All of this, enshrined in a very disarming humility, has made him a most attractive and lovable bearer of good tidings. He has a lot to teach anyone who wants to proclaim effectively the Good News.

****

Just before I came up here, Brother Luke gave me a tape of John Michael Talbot. I guess some might be a bit scandalized if they heard John Michael's strumming coming from the hermitage — just as they might have been by hearing Tom playing Dylan or Joan Baez. But these are the voices that are reaching the multitudes. Like his Father, Saint Francis, John Michael traverses the highways and byways proclaiming the Good News in his songs. As I listen to him, not only is my own spirit lifted up by the beauty of his voice, music, and message, but I walk with him and bring my love to his ministry. May the Lord make it abundantly fruitful. To many hurting hearers he brings the word of healing love, to hearts that might never hear such a word in a church. Would to God that in the renewal many of the sons of Saint Francis would abandon their big institutions and return to the streets and highways in the spirit of their Father. Our times need this troubadour of love far more than did the fourteenth century. I thank the Lord for John Michael and all the courageous young men and women like him who dare to receive and attempt to live the full spirit of Francis today.

****

In Isaiah, the Lord speaks of the slackness of his people and the keenness of the nations he summons to punish them. Would that apply today? Are we, his people, slack? Are those concerned about the things of the material world far more diligent? What of us contemplatives? Do we rest and take our ease? Or are we keen in our practice? As Saint Benedict asks, do we *truly* seek God? (The English word doesn't do justice to the intensity of its Latin root, *vere*.) Are we content to have already found him, touching but the hem of his robe? There, indeed, we have found healing, but should we not be pressing forward to follow him into the depths of the Paschal mystery? Do we sleep on Tabor and in the Garden? Or even remain outside in the valley? Chosen we are, yet fearful, keeping our distance, willing to hear him through others, rather than entering into the cloud, letting go of the security of all our familiar landmarks. Well did our fathers warn us so insistently of *accedia* — slackness of spirit. Lord, teach me how to be a complete "yes" without tension, but with total attention. Give me the grace to live what you teach.

****

The night seems to have grown warmer. Clouds hide all the stars. There is the muffled rumble of thunder from afar — unless it is still the artillery at Fort Knox. A great generator or perhaps a cooler at the Gethsemani Farms dominates the silence. A dog barks. A plane passes overhead. A truck passes on the road. A shot is heard in the distance. One does not seem to find silence in the knobs of Kentucky. Yes, I can understand why Tom wanted something more remote.

****

Thomas Merton's secretary, Brother Patrick Hart.

What is Thomas Merton's most significant contribution?

Dom James might say his obedience. Others might point to his prayer and contemplative life, while others would indicate his social concern. I think it is his freedom.

It stands out in the context of his obedience and makes that obedience true. It was his freedom that enabled him to be completely available to God in prayer and to be taken beyond himself in contemplation. His freedom opened him to let the whole world, with all its concerns and needs, walk in. His freedom from himself enabled him to remain open even when those concerns and the people who shared them — though often in a much less deep way than he — shredded him and left him tattered.

And what does Tom have to say to us?

He might say, "I really don't have anything to say. I don't have any answers. Live the questions." There is struggle — all the way. *Be free*!! Be yourself. How? By prayer. I don't mean saying prayers. I mean the kind of prayer where you leave all your thoughts and images behind, your phony self, and find your true self in God. At the same time, we find everybody else there. And we realize how we are all one in God, and everything else follows.

Thursday, December Fifth

The reading I had for lauds was from the words of our Lord's public ministry:

> "Now the hour has come for the Son of Man to be glorified. I tell you most solemnly, unless a grain of wheat falls in the ground and dies, it remains only a single grain. But if it dies, it yields a rich harvest. Anyone who loves his life loses it; anyone who hates his life in this world will keep it for eternal life."

I remember the Zen story of a terrible outlaw who was terrorizing villages. Whenever the people heard he was coming, they fled and left all for him. As he approached one village, everyone fled, except one monk. When the outlaw heard that the monk had remained in his monastery, he was outraged. He broke down the gates of the monastery and confronted the monk. "Do you know who I am?" I am the one who can kill you on the spot." The monk looked at him calmly and replied, "Do you know who I am? I am the one who can let you kill me on the spot."

Freedom!

Whatever decision I make about my future, I want to make it freely — free to let go or free to go on. Letting go of my life in this world — the life I live in the knowledge of the world through my writings, lectures, and activities, I may well find a greater freedom with the eternal life here and now. What more could I want? Falling to the ground — dying in the sight of the world, my life can become more fruitful. Is that what you want, Lord?

Is freedom to be found in saying "no" to what many ask and expect of me? Or should I be free enough to say "yes" without fear of losing anything of the contemplative reality of my own union with the Lord.

I pray the last words of the *Benedictus*:

Give light to those who live in darkness and the shadow
of death . . .
Guide our feet into the way of peace.

****

The monastic charism is a charism of freedom, including the
freedom not to count in the world, and not to give visible results
in it, the freedom not to have to talk if you don't want, not
to have to pronounce judgment on anything, or contrary-wise,
to speak out without hesitation when you think something has
to be said (not just when you think somebody else wants you
to say it for them). Above all, the monastic charism is a freedom
from set routine and official tasks. A monk does not have to
do any of these things. Not because he has a secret luxury
product for a somewhat esoteric market, but because he is
liberated from the need to produce anything with which to
justify himself in the eyes of other men. He is not accountable
to them for his life because it is something that cannot be drawn
up on a balance sheet for anybody's inspection. The "solitude"
of the monk is the loneliness of being accountable directly to
God for something that the monk does not quite understand
himself.

The "community" of the monk is not just his tidy little
cloistered family but the whole human family.

****

This is the day on which Tom last wrote me — a postcard
from Singapore, received just hours before the news of his death.
It was partly business, about the galleys for *The Climate of
Monastic Prayer*, which we were preparing for publication. He
was enthusiastic about Asia, as well he might have been after
Polonnaruwa. He concluded his note with ". . . and more yet
to come." Yes, so much more!

Some have thought that Tom had an intimation of his impending death. I think not. He was full of plans and life. Polonnaruwa was complete. Such experiences are. They fill all our potential. But in the very act of fulfilling us, they create yet more potency. *"He who eats this bread will hunger yet more."* One who has lived the Christian life for a time knows there is always more — and he expects it. This is why the contemplative life is never boring, but always high adventure when fully lived: There is always more!

In the pastures of plenty my soul lies down.
— Psalm 23:2

****

The clouds are beginning to drop down their moisture, the cistern at the side of the house gathers it. It seems to gather all the water needed. Yet, for safety's sake, the monks bring large milk cans of water from the monastery for drinking and cooking. Acid rain causes its concern even here. Is there anything among God's good gifts that we have not in some way abused? We even abuse his holy image, the child of God, in ourselves and in others. Lord, have mercy.

****

It has been good just being here quietly before the fire. I have pushed myself to pray the office and to do some reading. Mass is good.

The usual congregation of birds have been here for lunch: the nuthatch choosing the nuts; the blue jay, the biggest pieces of bread it can find; and Mr. and Mrs. Cardinal enjoying the seeds. The titmouse failed to show up.

****

As I was praying in the chapel I thought how different my life, and the lives of many others (perhaps millions), would be if Tom had never lived — and had not died. I wouldn't have had the good retreats that I have had in this hermitage. I wouldn't be writing a book about him. Thank God for Tom! And thank you, too, Lord for my own life. How different some people's lives would have been if there hadn't been a Basil. It is a humbling and great privilege to be used by God to make a difference in the life of another human being. It has eternal consequences.

****

Merton's review of *Ends and Means* in the *Columbia Review* in March of 1938 shows he was quite familiar with Huxley's work. The "new" he found in *Ends and Means* was the prominence of love — that is, the denial of ambition, self-assertion, and even the seemingly harmless exhibitionism inexorably called forth by a society where men are judged by their material possessions. In this insight received from Huxley Tom found a new freedom.

I think it would be difficult to exaggerate the impact that Huxley had on Tom. It may seem paradoxical that such an influence should have come from a secular prophet or a "rational idealist," as Huxley frequently called himself, but it was this rational idealism that not only spoke to Tom when he was young but enabled him in time to speak so powerfully to the young of the next generation as well as to his own contemporaries. However, with Tom, the idealism took an infinite step, into the realms of faith — there is the secret of his perduring power. His rationalism, not contrary but complementary to faith, remained in touch with and probed the real fabric of life, creating the realistic, hope-engendering connections between our everyday struggles, our very real humanness, and an ideal grand enough to enkindle the human heart. Tom took

Huxley's peace and love and elevated them to the all-embracing peace of Christ and Christ's total, transcendent love.

****

One of the things that has come to me more in my recent reading of Tom's writings is how much a philosopher he is. He really took the best of medieval philosophy, studying the masters, Aquinas and Scotus, with the help of Gilson, Maritain, and Walsh, and then read widely in the moderns, being most profoundly influenced by Gabriel Marcel. John Howard Griffin paints a rather humorous scene, right here in this hermitage. When Griffin brought the aged Jacques Maritain to visit Gethsemani, Tom invited the visitors up here and tried to open the old Thomist to some existentialist thinking by playing Bob Dylan's "Highway 61" for him — at top volume, notes Griffin. On the dedication page of *Raids on the Unspeakable* — a book that Tom considered different from all his other books and more to the point — Tom gives a quotation from Marcel, which I think sums up his own aspirations as a philosopher:

> "Today, the first and perhaps the only duty of the philosopher is to defend man against himself: to defend man against that extraordinary temptation toward inhumanity to which — almost without being aware of it — so many human beings today have yielded."

Berdyaev brings this insight to the level of faith and theology:

> "The practical conclusion dervied from eschatological faith turns into an accusation of the age in which I live and into a command to be human in this most inhuman of ages, to guard the image of man for it is the image of God."

****

79

A pair of hoot owls call to each other in the high pines behind the hermitage. It has grown warm, almost forty degrees, as clouds rest close to the earth. The hermitage is now too warm, as the fireplace throws off a lot of heat. It took several days to warm up the house, but now its cinder blocks have drunk in the daily fire and hold its warmth. I pray the psalms, listen to the sounds of night, watch the leaping flames, and praise God.

> Who neither ignored my prayer
> nor deprived me of his love.
>
> — Psalm 66:20

****

Awareness that is complete self-possession along with complete lack of self-consciousness depends on freedom from addiction to all the current mental narcotics, from the funny sheets to speeches about the constitution. Also, it depends on a certain detachment from the love of intellectual curiosity for its own sake.

****

Tomorrow I will begin to break my fast by observing the traditional monastic type of fast, taking one meal after Vespers (sundown). Sunday, the day of the Resurrection, I will not fast. I haven't noticed anything significant from these four days of fasting. But that is hardly a significant fast: four days. The most notable benefit has been in not having to bother preparing food and using time to eat. That in itself is a certain freedom.

Friday,

December

Sixth

Yahweh, the teacher of mankind,
knows exactly how we think,
how our thoughts are a puff of wind.

— Psalm 94:10

****

Today I will follow the old monastic fast, which was the fast
of the whole Christian community. It was observed by the
Trappists until the end of the last century. On Sundays and
feasts and during Easter time the monks ate at noon after
praying sext. On ordinary days they ate after none, around
2 p.m. On real fast days they waited till evening, eating after
vespers. In the 1890s, Pople Leo XIII forbade the monks to
fast past noon. So they started having sext earlier and eating
at 11 on feast days. On ordinary days they prayed none at
11 a.m. and ate at 11:30. And on fast days they crammed
virtually the whole office into the morning, celebrating vespers
at 11:15 and eating at 12 noon. It surely was a cram. For we
not only had the canonical office but also the office of the
Blessed Virgin and the office for the dead. On the Fridays of
Lent we threw in a procession with the penitential psalms and
the litany of the saints. Between 2 a.m., when we rose, and
noon — ten hours — we spent over six hours in choir, without
a bite to eat. No wonder many monks, like Tom, ended up
with stomach problems and lots of nervous tension. Of course,
the renewal has changed all that. The offices got back to their
proper times and the individual monk moderates his own fasting
with the guidance of his spiritual father. So today, with all
reverence to Leo XIII, this "Trappist" will fast till evening after
vespers.

****

I would say that the more conscious one is of "being a monk" the more the true monastic charism is likely to be stifled by a false consciousness. To be a monk one must learn to be a non-monk. It does require discipline, and a great deal of discipline. Not pseudo-discipline (the rote learning of minute prescriptions) but genuine radical re-formation.

****

Tom says that the desert was created simply to be itself, not to be transformed into something else. I am a bit surprised by this. It was prophesied that the desert would bloom. It did bloom in a real way when so many ardent Christians went to the desert and used its special environment as the milieu in which to blossom as men and women of God. But I don't think some of the wonderful achievements of the Israeli in making the desert fruitful are contrary to the divine plan. All things are ours and we are God's. We can use the desert in different ways. We monks must not be possessive of anything, not even the desert. Others can use it in different ways for the good of the human family and the glory of God. May we quickly learn how to use the deserts of Africa for our starving brothers and sisters there.

Always we have to beware of absolutes. Tom wrote of this in one of his letters, very strongly but humbly. He certainly was the foremost in proclaiming that there is more than one way to live the monastic life and even the Cistercian life. And there is more than one way to be an authentic hermit, living an authentic eremitical life. We are so prone to make our way the only way, our understanding the only right one.

We are even apt to tie ourselves up in knots. Tom writes in *Thoughts in Solitude*: "Too many ascetics fail to become great saints because their rules and ascetic practices have merely deadened their humanity instead of setting it free to develop richly in all its capacities under the influence of grace."

****

The rash bluejay just came up and knocked on the window to remind me that I had not put out any bread this morning for him and his feathered friends. It made an attempt at snowing during the night, a powdered-sugar coating. The sun, also, made its attempt — at shining. Now it is another gray-blue winter day, colder, its crisp air inviting.

****

Brother Anthony discreetly left a packet of mail at the door this morning. I don't seem to be able to escape from mail no matter where I go. Twenty letters from half a dozen countries: a loving word from Father Francis in his ashram in Kerala; a note from my aunt wondering if I am still alive — I failed to get a note off to her for her anniversary. The old memory is getting weaker.

****

Lord, help me to escape all superficiality, all phoniness, especially in my relationship with you, but also in everything.

I think this is one of the things most attractive about Tom. He was totally genuine, or at least trying to be, trying to get completely free from the false ego, the phony self we so deeply identify with and so carefully protect for so many years. I think of some of the pictures of Tom from his college days — the put-on sophistication of his three-piece suits (I still wear a three-piece suit!), his fedora worn at a rakish angle, the cigarette dangling from his lips. He certainly bought into the false self, the projected image. Yet that something genuine, deep within him, finally won out. He went through the image of the monk before that happened. How many of us, especially we Cistercians, or even more those who hang onto the label of Trappist, get caught in the image of a monk.

When Father Flavian was elected abbot, Tom felt a new freedom. He publicly proclaimed to the community, "I am a professionally scandalous person. I do all sorts of crazy things." He wasn't saying this is the way we all should act. We all do need to find a freedom to be truly ourselves. The true self is the only thing that is real. This is the only thing that can glorify God, not any pretense or put-on performance of a monk. This is the only real gift we can give each other. Anything else is phony — not worth giving. If we are going to be a sacrament of God's love to each other, then we have to be the sacrament, the expression of his love, which he himself is creating and not something we are fabricating on our own. The only real gift I can give you is who I really am. Here it is; it is yours. Take it or leave it. It is all I have to give. It may not meet your expectations, your image of the "good monk." It may not be much of a monk at all, but it is what it is. Being true to itself, it can be an expression and channel of God's love. That doesn't mean that I shouldn't strive to be a better person, a better Christian, a better monk — for that is my vocation — but I shouldn't pretend to be what I am not yet.

****

We are essentially called to the unknown: "Eye has not seen, nor ear heard, nor has it entered into the human heart what God has prepared for those who love him." So we shouldn't be surprised if we find ourselves "in the dark." It is going to be difficult, if not impossible, to know for sure we are on the right path. In *Thoughts* Tom prays:

> My Lord God, I have no idea where I am going. I do not see the road ahead of me. I cannot know for certain where it will end. Nor do I really know myself, and the fact that I think that I am following your will does not mean that I am actually doing so.

But he goes on to add:

> But I believe that the desire to please you does in fact please you. And I hope I have that desire in all that I am doing. I hope that I will never do anything apart from that desire. And I know that if I do this, you will lead me by the right road though I may know nothing about it. Therefore will I trust you always though I may seem to be lost and in the shadow of death. I will not fear, for you are ever with me, and you will never leave me to face my perils alone.

A very consoling prayer.

We do have one way of judging whether we are truly walking in the way the Lord wants for us. Jesus said that we can judge a tree by its fruits. If the path we are following brings forth in us the fruits of the Spirit, those wonderful fruits Paul lists in his letter to the Galatians (love, peace, joy, kindness, long-suffering, meekness, mildness, and chastity), we can be sure we are walking in the way of the Lord. Such fruits do not come from our poor human efforts; they are a gift from the Lord.

****

Being united to God, entering more fully into the experience of that union through prayer, is supposed to do something to us. We are not always comfortable with that transforming power. We tend to cling to what we have experienced ourselves having and being. But if we want to get to our deepest self, we have to go to the place where it originates. If we want to experience our deeper self, we have to experience the place of our origin and that is something ever new. For God ever calls us forth from nothingness. We have to be willing to experience our nothingness, the *nada* of John of the Cross, to be able to come to the experience of the call of God which is the core of our being, the deepest self, our person at its roots. Furthermore, because we have sinned, we have to realize that we are called not only out of nothingness, but more importantly, out of sinfulness as well. If we are willing to experience our sinfulness, we can then truly experience Christ as our Saviour and know deeply the joy of salvation. Experience it,

not just know it in our heads and pay lip service to it; but experience actually being called out of nothingness and sinfulness. We want to have the consciousness that this is who we truly are. These two experiences, negative and painful though they may be, are the beginning of our experience of God, who is capable of calling us from nothingness and sin and bringing us to perfection so that we can, indeed, be perfect even as our heavenly Father is perfect. This depends on faith in God and hope in his mercy and love. Without faith and hope we cannot face our own nothingness and sinfulness, because this is so contrary to our instincts for self-preservation. The image of our own nothingness opens to us an abyss that is truly frightening — we don't know where it will bring us, but we are asked to live by faith.

There are a lot of things about our lives that we cannot bear, until they are upon us, for it is in that moment that we receive the grace to handle them. There is no master who has it all put together. Not even our Lord Jesus, our Master. The Scriptures tell us he learned by what he suffered, in the desert, in Gethsemani, and on the Cross. The only way we become true masters is the way Jesus did, by resurrection from the dead. That is the only way. We have to die to the false self, in order to live in the fullness of our Christ person.

****

If we are going to be what the Church wants us to be as contemplatives, we have to be willing to enter into contemplation — to die to ourselves, our own ideas, our own projects, our own doings, and open to God. The Second Vatican Council was a call to authenticity, to be what we are called. For it is not enough for us to be observant; it is not enough to say prayers and attend offices. We have to seek into the contemplative experience. We need to be constantly reminded of this and encouraged and strengthened to do it. Pep talks by the abbot are not enough. We need real guidance and life structures that foster and support this. Father Louis gives us good guidance and support in his writings and the witness of his fidelity. If our community is not supporting us in this, it is failing as a contemplative community. It is failing us and it is failing the Church.

We need companions on the way and we need guides. We do not, in fact, *hear* much that we are told when we first encounter it — in either the spoken or written word — because we are not there yet. We can absorb so little at a time. We need companions and guides who repeat what we have heard, perhaps many, many times, until the moment when we can finally hear it, when we need to hear it. We also need companions and guides to *encourage* us. Because it takes courage to live up to what we hear, to do that to which we are called. It is very lonely, the encounter with the nothingness and sin from which we come. But we must go through this to come to the experience of the true self, which is the self in communion and union with God and all others.

None of us is meant to engage this process alone. "It is not good for man [or woman] to be alone," was one of the Lord's first reflections on his creation. That is why we are called into community, the Christian community of the people of God and also particular communities of home, family, monastery. We are in our communities to encourage and support one another in this, respecting what God is doing in each one and the pace he adopts, being supportive without being intrusive. Even hermits need this in some ways — at least, they need spiritual fathers and/or mothers. Often a hermit is helped and encouraged by those who come seeking help.

We need to be willing to expose ourselves, our needs, beyond the armor and shell of our socialized selves.

****

Religion means having a relationship — again to be "bound up" with — a relationship with the living God. This is the *raison*

d'etre of all that we do and are. A relationship with God, living,
personal, true, good, unlimited goodness, not only in himself
but toward us, for he is our creator (do we realize what that
means?), our goodness, and our happiness. Contemplation is
the summit of all human actions because it is the most total
relationship with God. It is exalted above all other human
activities. It is the thing that ultimately motivates, grounds, and
gives meaning to all else that we do as Christians.

****

The sun has finally won out, at least as much as a winter sun
can. The snow has disappeared. The distant knobs lie in their
mystic mist. The nuthatch has just arrived for lunch, followed
by the red-bellied pecker. They should be grateful to the jay,
who got me to serve up the meal. The cardinals have now
arrived, and the titmouse too. It is good to see and feel the sun.

****

I took a long walk this afternoon. The piety of a former time
seems to have put a shrine on the top of each surrounding knob:
Calvary, Saint Joseph, and so forth. And numerous shrines along
the way. As I looked back at the abbey from across the way,
I became aware of the old enclosure wall. It is easy to see how
Tom found it so confining in the early days when the monks
were allowed to go outside those walls only for work. In Europe
where villages encroached on the abbeys, that kind of enclosure
made sense, but not here where there are only acres and acres
of woodlands surrounding the Abbey. We never got around
to building enclosure walls at Spencer, so I never had the
experience of living within the walls until I lived for a time
in a European monastery. It must have seemed so unreasonable
to Tom to keep the two hundred monks packed together within
that confined space all the time. He certainly made enough

efforts to get that changed — with ultimate success.

The picnic ground at Saint Bernard's Lake is very much as it was in the days when Tom frolicked there with his many friends. The ducks came up quickly out of the water in hopeful expectation. Unfortunately, I had not thought to bring any bread or grain for them. I easily could have as I passed through the farm yard on my way out and there was a lot of grain about. I went on through the woods and climbed the steep knob to the watch tower. Tom once whimsically thought the tower would make a good hermitage. The trees have grown high around it; though it is a hundred feet, it is still difficult to see the abbey through the bare branches. I was only up there a short time when two men came through the woods and clambered up the ninety steps. I again felt a surge of sympathy for Tom and his quest for more solitude.

****

I sit in the chapel. There is the Presence in the icons. There is the Presence in the tabernacle. There is the Presence in the Mass. There is the Presence within — transcendent, yet immanent. My poor mind can struggle with all these Presences, but something deep within cuts through all and it is present. This is the only thing that satisfies, yet it doesn't satisfy. It isn't a question of satisfaction. There is no "I" to be satisfied. It just *is.* Yet it is not yet the eternal IS.

Why do I write all these words? They don't really say what I want to say. I am a word maker. It makes money for the Abbey. It is better than making Trappist Preserves — at least I would prefer to make words than jelly. More important, these words sometimes say something to my sisters and brothers whom I don't know but whom I love. I have prayed for them all in this chapel at Mass today — all who will read these words that I am writing during this retreat — if they ever get read. The Lord God seems to use my words in some way to speak to those whom he loves. What else would I want but that the Lord use me as an instrument of his love. All I have is his gift. The more he uses it, the better. And if it is his good pleasure not to use it, but let it be but a pleasure in his sight, all the better. Lord, I am all yours; at least I want to be all yours. Let not the vagaries of my poor heart stray from you.

> We ruin our life of prayer if we are constantly examining our prayer and seeking the fruit of prayer in a peace that is nothing more than a psychological process. The only thing to seek in contemplative prayer is God; and we seek him successfully when we realize that we cannot find him unless he shows himself to us, and yet at the same time he would not have inspired us to seek him unless we had already found him.
>
> — *Thoughts in Solitude*

Saturday, December Seventh

The sun is rising. A jogger goes pounding along the edge of the woods. The birds are singing their many songs and will soon be coming for breakfast. I decided not to fast today, partly because of the feast, the Immaculate Conception of the Blessed Virgin Mary, partly because I have become too tired and would not be able to function. It is probably a conjunction of the fast and the long hike yesterday. I usually wake up automatically after five hours of sleep, but this morning I slept till after six.

The Feast of the Immaculate Conception of Mary has been transferred to today. The year Tom died it was celebrated on the Sunday, but we don't do that anymore. This is our national patronal feast. It is also the patronal feast of my home diocese and of the seminary where I studied. May Mary watch over the nation and give us a new beginning of peace. May she bless Brooklyn and its good bishop and all those who were with me at the seminary. The feast bespeaks an innocence that only God can give. That is something we so much need, a new beginning, first of all in our own lives, so that we can make a new beginning as a human family, loving, trusting, and caring for each other all throughout this nation and throughout this globe of ours, the shared home of us all.

Because it is the seventh, it is also the anniversary of the attack on Pearl Harbor, which catapulted Tom into Gethsemani. He may have gotten here anyway some weeks later. But it is interesting to see that that nefarious event in some way initiated a powerful spiritual force in our nation. God does bring good out of evil.

Today is also the anniversary of my father's death, thirty years before Tom's. I guess parents in some way transmit to their children their hope and aspiration that their lives will make a difference. Tom's mother, like my father, did not live long. Her heritage was two sons. Owen Merton left some fine paintings, but few know them and fewer prize them. John Paul Merton, Tom's brother, died so young. But the family can indeed be proud of the heritage they left in Tom. He did make a difference and continues to make a difference in the lives of many and in the thinking of the nation. I am sure he is more than a little responsible for the recent peace pastoral of the American bishops. Many of the bishops have been formed at least in part by his writings. They have heard his words and those words have borne fruit.

****

So here I am, wasting time, watching fire licking the dark and then watching cardinals eating their breakfast. I guess many a monsignor has had the privilege of watching as a cardinal ate his breakfast — but I fear his contemplation may have been vitiated by a bit of ambition. I can hope for no promotions from my cardinals, just the sheer joy of watching them. So rarely do we contemplate reality and just let it be with us in communion. That is just a waste of time! A waste that delights our Maker and glorifies him. In a conference that Father Louis gave to the novices on T.S. Eliot's "Little Gidding," he warned them against the fruitless and unprofitable task of trying always to put a finger on the meaning of things. We need to let things be and be with us in their being and not always strain them through our poor concepts.

****

The fluorescent light is impossible. It has nothing to do with prayer. It is cold and noisy, a blatant intrusion. Compare it with the diffuse lighting of a Romanesque church, descending as it were from heaven, or the translucent effect achieved in the Gothic. The modern concept of a building is of a machine within which to operate: a practical, functional, active entity around us, adapting the environment to our desires. To what extent do we want our churches or our homes or our monasteries to be machines in which the light can be arranged for the function and be the same, day and night? It is a different approach to life, an artificial one, which can lead to artificial living. We have lost sight of the value of an environment which flows from nature. On Mount Athos, there was never any electric light in the churches, even when it was in the monasteries — which was rare, though I am told that that is rapidly changing. The Church as a place of prayer does better to mediate the natural rhythm of the world, not only with its light and dark, but with the sounds of its times and its seasons: the rain on the roof, the wind blowing through the arches, the birds at dawn, and the stillness of the evening. We are so unconscious of our environment. Even of the human environment. We stick our noses into the little books we now have in choir and are there almost as solitary individuals, so much less part of the choir than we used to be when we sang together

from our large Latin choir books. I hope we will some day produce such magnificent books for the new English language liturgy. So many of the ceremonies were really choir ceremonies before the servant of the Church did this, the hebdomidary said that, the reader did the other part. So different from the idea of saying office on one's own or the obligation of the office which active religious have. For us it is rather a community project, a common celebration. We are in danger of losing so much of that. We need to be more aware of how the little things of ceremony and ritual create the environment that supports this important reality.

****

While the gruff jay gobbles up great hunks of bread or grabs them and flies off, the lady cardinal gently pecks at a modest scrap of bread or some small seeds and never carries anything away from the table. A titmouse has just landed on the window frame, almost knocking himself out on the glass. He eyes me now with intense curiosity. His tuft makes him look like a wide-eyed adolescent. He taps tentatively on the glass with his beak, not sure what to make of it. His eyes and his head are in almost constant motion, taking in every aspect. His tuft rises as tension grows and relaxes as he relaxes. I feel sorry for these little ones who must live in such constant fear. A big jay swoops in and the little fellow flies away.

Mr. Cardinal is certainly more striking than Mrs. But Mrs. is the more beautiful. The many hues shading through her plumage make up a miracle of coloring.

A pair of juncos have joined the congregation this morning. I don't think I have ever seen one before. It is good that there is a book here to identify my guests.

****

I climbed to the top of a high knob, northwest of the Abbey. There is a magnificent view of the whole monastery. I could also see the hermitage in the pine grove. When they dismantled the great silver spire, Tom wasn't happy about the change. He told the novices it left the church looking like one of the barrel factories in the area. They mounted the cross that stood atop it on the summit of the knob. Unfortunately the cross has toppled over and it now lies in ruins, the metal veneer peeling off the well-seasoned timber. The great silver spire — how many memories it evokes.

On my way back I stopped at the Gethsemani shrine in the cedar grove near the road. The fine sculptures were erected in memory of Jonathan M. Daniel, an Episcopal seminarian from Boston who died a martyr for freedom in Alabama on

the very day that Tom left the community for the hermitage, August 20, 1965. Tom felt a deep solidarity with this young man and many others, like Martin Luther King, Jr., who died in the cause of freedom, freedom from oppression in a country that is built on freedom and proclaims it for all, and yet still allows so much oppression. Plans had been made for King to be with Tom at Gethsemani the very day he was shot. An unfortunate change in those plans put off his visit. The mysterious ways of Providence. This fact only bound Tom more deeply to the struggle for freedom.

****

Of Father Louis's Gethsemani, one might say only the skeleton remains. The dormitory, where he struggled with insomnia for so many nights, is now a long row of private cells. The vault where he first found some private space to work is now a lightsome secretary's office (inhabited by the brother who last served him as secretary — Patrick Hart, now the abbot's secretary). His novitiate is gone, replaced by a new novitiate (with few) and an infirmary (with many), commanding a magnificent view over the knobs in the direction of Tom's hermitage. The great silver spire that welcomed him as he approached the Abbey that first night in the spring of 1941 has been exiled to a woody knob. The many graves around the apse of the church — witnesses of his earliest attempts to find a bit of solitude and to write some poetry — still stand in their crowded array, too crowded to find room for him. He, rather, lies — no longer alone — under the handsome spreading spruce to the side of the renewed church and its added sacristy. The cloister garth is now like a city square with modern street lamps, potted flowers, and a gentle, almost Zen-like fountain, surrounded by an austere, concrete cloister walk. It is a different place and yet so truly the same, inhabited by many of the men Father Louis so deeply loved, many of whom he guided as they took their first steps along those cloisters.

This is a place where prayer has been valid. There have

been saints here. Perhaps not according to the popular taste. Saints perhaps in spite of everything. That is the way that it is. It goes back to God. God has done it this way.

> Yahweh, what variety you have created,
> arranging everything so wisely.
>
> — Psalm 104:24

****

What was Mary's life like up to the time of the Annunciation? Undoubtedly a life of quiet fidelity. But a fidelity to the ordinary. So ordinary that she herself did not perceive its absolute uniqueness: she, alone, the sinless one. So when Gabriel swept in, she did not know what to make of his expression of God's particular favor in her regard. Holiness, for almost all of us almost all of the time, lies in the ordinary. The moments of annunciation, the call to the extra-ordinary, are rare. If we are destined for such a moment, we can be sure that we are going to be ready for it *only* if we are, here and now, day in and day out, faithful to the ordinary. Monastic life, spiritual life, Christ-life, consists in the everyday stuff, not living out some fantastic ideal we have conceived. By being really with what is going on around us, by being present to each person who walks in our door, by being who we really are, we experience the presence of God here and now. Mary was ready: "Behold the handmaid of the Lord." With her help we can be ready.

****

In his teaching to the novices on chastity, Father Louis's emphasis was on freedom, according to Romans 7. The Holy Spirit, the Spirit of Freedom, enables us to live in his Spirit. If we give ourselves over to the deep life forces in our nature, we lose something of our freedom, being driven by them and bound by the consequences.

I am struck at how sacred is the generative power within us and our faculties to express it. What a disreverence to manipulate this in any way. We do not have enough reverence for our bodies, the exquisite beauty of this expression of God's creative love. I can only use the word *sacred,* for I am touched with awe. The word of the psalmist comes to mind: "I thank you, God, for the wonder of my being."

****

Your whole life consists in burning bridges behind you.
— Thomas Merton

There should be a continuity of burnt bridges. The crises in our lives burn up the love that holds us in this world; we are set free, and then we can hear the Word of God.

****

Evening is settling in. It is part of the tender quality time. Even when a low cloud-cover uniformly hides the sun and allows for none of the rich display of autumn sunsets. It is winter. The active fire in the hearth is more of a comfort now. But still, I do not want to miss the quality of this time of day, which calls us to vespers more surely than the Abbey bell. It bespeaks a day done — for better or worse it is done, slipping into the darkness of the eternal now. We will see it again when we slip over and meet all our days in the mercy of God. For now, even though there is some wanting, feeling that we have let some of or much of the day's potential evade us, it is good that it is evening and that the day is slipping away. We have had enough of it for now. How good is our God to give us these alternations of light and dark, of the succeeding seasons.

The loblolly pines stand out now against the misty ridges, each one's particular beauty etched more clearly. Hedgerow blends into woods, fields into hedgerow. Now the great bell of the Abbey makes its proclamation. The monks have gathered in choir. It is time for vespers.

****

Mrs. Cardinal is on the porch again, for some supper, more courageous in the darkening shadows. Now the red-bellied woodpecker joins her. He seems so crippled when he tries to stand on the horizontal — he is meant to cling to the vertical. The Lord prepares us so well for the tasks he has for us — if only we can see what they are and stick to them.

****

Tom has given me quite a few conferences this week. I listened to a number of his tapes. In fact, I don't think I want to hear his voice again for a while. He is good. There is such a blend of lighthearted humor and profound insight. His method is Socratic. While he waits for the novices to reply, I try to answer myself. It is engaging. We have looked at freedom and chastity, at social issues and monastic attitudes, at contemporary events and world-shaking happenings. It has been a rich diet, leaving much yet to be digested. He has been a good retreat master — challenging.

His message is basically catholic: we must have a catholic heart — a universal heart. All things and persons are ours and we are Christ's and Christ is God's. It is as simple as that. We live the Paschal Mystery with Christ to be transformed ourselves into the fullness of our Christ person and to bring all to the Father with Christ. That is the sum total of it.

What does that mean in everyday living?

First of all it means enough prayer and meditation and contemplation to keep constantly aware, to live out of the Center, to be free to come and go from the Center, from the creative source of our being, open and ready for all the surprises of God.

It means in that awareness, in the strength of that grace, to be a "yes" to all that is in God and in each one who walks into our lives in each event, letting the fullness of the person feed us and rest us and rejoice us. I fear clutter. But there is no clutter when each thing is welcomed this way. Things, projects, even people (Lord, have mercy!) become clutter when they are not seen and welcomed as manifestations in the Presence, but are allowed just to crowd into the limited space of our lives.

****

Above my desk at home there is a picture that the priests at Saint Luke's gave me when I shared the Centering Prayer with them. It shows two seals rubbing noses. The caption is "K.I.S.S. — Keep it Simple, Stupid." That is the thing I have to keep in mind. Simplicity: being fully to the reality of each day with a plan but free enough to disregard the plan to be responsive to what God allows.

Sunday, December Eighth

This is the day Tom wrote his last entry in his personal journal. He was about to enter fully into the conference at Bangkok. He would not make time the next two days to write. And this will be my last journal entry here in his hermitage.

It has been a good time, a blessed time. It has really been a time with Tom, through his tapes and his books and more through his spiritual presence here, in these woods and in this cottage. But most of all, in the reality of which he wrote so well: in that place in the "now" of God, which is no place but where we are all of us together now in God.

So what is Tom's message for us?

As I sit here before the fire, or walk in the woods, or pray before the icons in the chapel, enjoying the "life free from care," I think that is (as he stated to the community on the day he came up here) his message: live a life free from care. Of course, we can't all have a carefree life. But we can at least move in that direction. We fill our lives with so many unnecessary cares — even we monks. When the monks here were changing over to private cells, Tom urged them to build them as places of prayer and to think of them that way and not as places to establish a private kingdom of which they would have all the care. How much we all tend to clutter our lives with things and projects we don't really need — and then we have to take care of them. I am impressed at how simple Tom kept his hermitage. It is a model of Cistercian simplicity: just the essentials with gracious space, like the great twelfth-century abbeys, but definitely twentieth-century, with cinder block and aluminum frame windows. It bothers me that Tom let fluorescent bars be put in the main room — such a cold and noisy mode of lighting. I suppose he rarely used them. In the *Geography of Lograire* he wrote of the arrival of electricity here: "I have chosen electric life in spades." And when he got his tape recorder, he added: "Conscience is a bronco well busted, memory secured by electric tape."

I look at the clutter of my own life. That is really what

is at issue. I have to learn to say "no" to the little things that clutter: the book reviews and prefaces, the talks to students and ladies' guilds. The gardening is OK; I need the fresh air and exercise. But I have to avoid other projects. If I can get a handle on the clutter and the correspondence, my life could be a bit more free. Still, something more radical than that is perhaps needed, at least for a while. As Tom says in his *Thoughts in Solitude*, to be a person implies freedom and responsibility. Both of these call for a certain interior solitude. But a cluttered or too full life — full of activities and concerns — leaves little interior solitude. Most people are, in fact, afraid of facing their own interior solitude. They flee from it, deliberately filling their lives with people, if they can, and with things. And in so doing they lose their freedom and become irresponsible — not responsible to many of the basic human needs around them and even in their own lives. They become addictively dependent on their chosen clutter. I am told that the average American allows television to fill a quarter of his time. What an investment of life! One of the reasons Tom was able to accomplish so much was that he was free from television and spectator sports. He preferred to play life's game rather than watch others play it. He didn't watch the Vietnam War or the race riots on TV. He heard about them, prayed, and acted, doing all he could to bring healing and peace. An uncluttered life gives a lot more freedom to be a responsive person.

So what am I going to do?

It seems to me pretty clear that I shall not accept any commitments after July and take a period of quiet for the rest of the year. Also, I will not let the first part of the year get any more cluttered. Then about this time next year I can decide what to do after that.

And what does Tom have to say?

Above all: Be free! Be love!

And where is freedom found?

In prayer. Not in saying prayers, but in that kind of prayer that touches God at the ground of our being, where we are one with him and one with our true selves and with all others.

We need to be free from ourselves, from our false selves, projections and images, so that we can be open to reality in ourselves and in others. Right living will necessarily follow from true love and deep prayer.

Our communities need to be free from trying to maintain some kind of Trappist or contemplative image. Free to be, in the fullest way possible, an environment that fosters true contemplation. Let reality be first — and that exists only in individuals — and let that determine the structures and the observances. And let the whole Church find freedom. Freedom to be and to proclaim the love of Jesus Christ for all persons. Let us not be so concerned about protecting dogmas and distinguishing ourselves from others. Let us give witness to the universal care and compassion of the Crucified.

To him be all glory, forever and ever. Amen.